LIVING LEGACIES

*Ireland's National Historic Properties
in the care of the OPW*

Le ceannach díreach ó
FOILSEACHÁIN RIALTAIS,
52 FAICHE STIABHNA, BAILE ÁTHA CLIATH 2
(Teil: 01 – 0761106834 nó 1890 213434; Fax 0761106843)
nó trí aon díoltóir leabhar.

——————

To be purchased from
GOVERNMENT PUBLICATIONS,
52 ST. STEPHEN'S GREEN, DUBLIN 2.
(Tel: 0761106834 or 1890 213434; Fax: 0761106843) or
through any bookseller.

Contents

Director's Introduction 4
CARLOW, Altamont House & Gardens 7
CORK, Annes Grove 11
CORK, Doneraile Court 15
CORK, Fota Arboretum & Gardens 19
CORK, Ilnacullin / Garinish Island 23
DONEGAL, The Glebe Art Museum 29
DUBLIN, Áras an Uachtaráin 35
DUBLIN, Arbour Hill 41
DUBLIN, Dublin Castle 45
DUBLIN, Farmleigh 51
DUBLIN, Grangegorman Military Cemetery 57
DUBLIN, Irish National War Memorial Gardens 61
DUBLIN, National Botanic Gardens of Ireland 67
DUBLIN, Rathfarnham Castle 73
DUBLIN, St Enda's Park & the Pearse Museum 79
DUBLIN, St Stephen's Green Park 85
DUBLIN, The Casino at Marino 91
DUBLIN, The Garden of Remembrance 97
DUBLIN, The Iveagh Gardens 101
DUBLIN, The Phoenix Park 107
DUBLIN, The Royal Hospital, Kilmainham 113
KERRY, Derrynane House & Gardens 119
KERRY, The Great Blasket Island & Visitor Centre 125
KILDARE, Castletown 129
KILKENNY, Kilkenny Castle 135
LAOIS, Emo Court 141
LAOIS, Heywood Gardens 147
MEATH, Oldbridge House & the Battle of the Boyne Visitor Centre 151
WEXFORD, John F. Kennedy Arboretum 155
WICKLOW, National Botanic Gardens, Kilmacurragh 159
BELGIUM, The Island of Ireland Peace Park 165
Photo Credits 168

Director's Introduction

It gives me great pleasure, on behalf of the Commissioners of Public Works in Ireland, to introduce to you *Living Legacies: Ireland's National Historic Properties in the care of the OPW*, a visitor's guide to the extraordinary portfolio of historic properties that are managed and presented to visitors by the Office of Public Works (OPW).

Ireland's national heritage encompasses a diverse range of properties and places that embody thousands of years of our nation's history. Although much of our built heritage remains in private ownership, the state, through the OPW, cares for many properties that are central to our nation's past, or are important national and international exemplars of architecture, landscape design and collections. While many of these fine buildings and properties are home to our National Cultural Institutions, government departments and other state bodies, this book looks specifically at thirty-one properties and their associated collections that are cared for, managed and presented to the public through the OPW's National Historic Properties division.

From Dublin Castle to the Great Blasket Island, from the National Botanic Gardens to the Glebe Art Museum, each property has its own legacy and story, and fulfils a unique living function today for Irish citizens and international visitors alike. Over 3.5 million people visited this range

of properties in 2016 and alongside our core work in presenting the properties to the public, OPW staff manage ongoing programmes of conservation and restoration; research and publication; collections management; exhibitions; education; outreach; conferencing and cultural programming. As a result, these historic properties are vibrant places celebrating our rich cultural heritage, but also reflecting contemporary society through their modern usage and ongoing public engagement.

As we protect and manage the national patrimony, we celebrate the past patrons of these properties and, in particular, their dedicated cultivation and curation of these special places now in our care. We hope that we present these personal stories in a way that preserves and communicates the unique personality of each property.

I extend my sincere thanks to our research team based at Dublin Castle, in particular Dr Myles Campbell and William Derham, who have collated and edited this publication. My thanks also to Jurga Rakauskaite for her beautiful design work and to Mary Heffernan for her energy and dedication in bringing this publication to fruition. We are ever grateful to John Cahill APA and his architectural conservation team who share with us the commitment to presenting all of these properties to the very highest standards.

We are grateful too for the support of Commissioner John McMahon and his passion for, and unwavering commitment to, the entire Heritage estate in OPW's care. Finally, my heartfelt thanks to the Management Team - Margaret Gormley, Mary Heffernan, Dr Matthew Jebb and Dr Eugene Keane - and to all my colleagues in National Historic Properties who, through their rich skills and expertise, breathe new life into these great properties and are central to the warm, engaging experiences our visitors enjoy today.

It is timely that we present this guide in 2018 as we mark the European Year of Cultural Heritage, a European Union initiative to celebrate our diverse and shared cultural heritage throughout Europe. A core principle of this initiative is the idea that our heritage is not only preserved through our appreciation of it, but that it actually 'evolves through our engagement with it'. I hope that this publication will inspire you, in 2018 and beyond, to visit, explore and enjoy these unique places and in doing so, to help shape that evolution. We look forward to welcoming you to one of Ireland's National Historic Properties in the near future.

Rosemary Collier
Director,
National Historic Properties

ALTAMONT
HOUSE
&
GARDENS

*A romantic garden paradise born of a
Carlow family tradition*

COUNTY CARLOW

Text by:
William
Derham

On the banks of the River Slaney in Co. Carlow, in a glen carved out of the landscape during the last ice age, lies the Altamont estate, which contains one of the finest gardens in Ireland.

Altamont House was constructed in the 1720s, incorporating parts of an earlier structure said to have been a medieval nunnery. In the 1850s, a lake was excavated in the grounds of the House, but it was when the Lecky-Watsons, a local Quaker family, acquired Altamont in 1924 that the Gardens truly came into their own.

Feilding Lecky-Watson had worked as a tea planter in Ceylon (Sri Lanka), where he nurtured his love of exotic plants, and of rhododendrons in particular. Back in Ireland, he became an expert in the species, cultivating plants for the botanical gardens at Glasnevin, Kew and Edinburgh. So passionate was he about these plants that when his wife, Isobel, gave birth to a daughter in 1922, she was named Corona, after his favourite variety of rhododendron.

Corona grew up sharing her father's passion and enthusiasm for plants and following the Second World War, took over the running of the Altamont demesne from her parents. In 1965, she held a party at Altamont, at which guests skated on the great lake, which had frozen over. One of the guests, Colonel Gary North, caught her eye. The following year they were married and the couple moved into the keeper's cottage. Between this cottage and the main House, Corona created a ribbon arboretum and a bog garden. Following her mother's death, aged 101, Corona North and her husband moved into Altamont House itself.

The gardens at Altamont are largely the triumph of one woman's struggle against the constant creep of nature. In the formal garden adjacent to the House stands a giant deodar cedar, beneath which runs the broad walk that leads from the House to the lake. This is lined with clipped yews and box hedges, to either side of which Corona planted rose beds. She also laid out a wisteria walk and a peony walk.

Around the lake, there are mature conifers that were planted in the 1800s, including a giant wellingtonia that commemorates the Battle of Waterloo. Under these trees Corona continued her father's planting of rhododendrons, for which she shared an equal passion, adding magnolias and Japanese maples. In a glen of sessile oaks, she planted hollies, Chilean fire trees, ferns and rare camellias. Another feature, 'the 100 steps', hand-cut in granite, lead down to the River Slaney.

The gardens and walks also encouraged the animal life that Corona cared so deeply about – red squirrels in the wooded areas, otters in the lake and river, and a variety of chickens and fowl, including peacocks, which added yet more to Altamont's attractions.

Altamont was a labour of love for Corona North. She once commented: 'I just do all this because I want the garden to continue'. In this spirit, she opened Altamont to thousands of visitors each year, and ran classes and courses. Accordingly, it became one of Ireland's premier gardens, attracting visitors from around the globe. Before her death in 1999, she made preparations to hand Altamont over to the Irish state to ensure its preservation.

Since Altamont was taken into state care, the OPW has worked hard to preserve the grounds and to continue the work that Corona was so passionate about. Visitors still come to see the wild daffodils, the bluebells and the snowdrops, and to lose themselves in the gardens and walks that make Altamont such an enchanting place to visit.

ALTAMONT HOUSE & GARDENS

Bunclody Road
Altamont
Ballon
Co. Carlow

General Enquiries
+353 (0) 59 915 9444
altamontgardens@opw.ie
www.heritageireland.ie

ANNES GROVE

A lush garden haven on the banks of the River Awbeg

COUNTY CORK

Text by:
*Hugh
Carrigan*

Previous page
A RUSTIC BRIDGE
IN THE GARDENS

THE QUEEN ANNE
HOUSE AT ANNES
GROVE

THE ORNAMENTAL
LILY POND

Nestled into an eighteenth-century ornamental glen, adjacent to the River Awbeg, the demesne of Annes Grove in north Co. Cork is the setting for the most exquisite Robinsonian-style gardens in Ireland. That style, championed by the nineteenth-century garden writer William Robinson, is characterized by the planting of a mixture of native and exotic species in a naturalized setting. In tandem with the work of Gertrude Jekyll, Robinson's approach helped to bring about a major shift in garden design, away from the excesses of Victorian formality towards simpler, more natural styles. Together with the early eighteenth-century Queen Anne house and outbuildings at Annes Grove, as well as the adjacent home farm, these significant Robinsonian gardens complete a designed demesne landscape that is unique in Ireland.

The Gardens at Annes Grove were largely the creation of Richard Grove Annesley in the first half of the twentieth century. Blessed with pockets of acid and alkaline soil, they accommodate an unusually wide range of plants. In developing this botanical cornucopia, Annesley used a canopy of native species to provide a backdrop for the exotic planting he introduced.

Today, Annesley's Gardens are of international significance, primarily because of their famous plant collection, which contains an outstanding range of rhododendron species. Among the most significant rhododendrons are specimens raised by Annesley from seed collected in Nepal and Tibet by the influential botanist Frank Kingdon-Ward. As a co-sponsor of Kingdon-Ward's plant-hunting expeditions,

Annesley was also able to acquire a significant collection of azaleas, which remain a highlight of the visitor experience. Other significant plants in the collection include the Tibetan cowslip and the Himalayan poppy.

At the centre of the walled garden, a fully restored Gothic-style summerhouse offers a captivating vista. Among the features to be enjoyed from here, are the intricate curved box hedges known as ribbon beds. A little distance away, two long herbaceous borders provide bursts of colour in shades of pink and blue. As silver and pink stachys tumble onto the stone flags, tall pink and white phlox, cannas and thalictrum take up the rear and provide height. Pergolas knotted with wisteria, honeysuckle and roses stretch out from these double borders, leading through a shaded woody walk, under cherry and eucryphia, to a lily pond.

Beyond the water, the path meanders into the shade of a Victorian stone fernery. This is an arrangement of natural-looking stone ledges and mounds built to house a collection of ferns. Like the ferns, it holds moisture and glistens after the rain, giving this dark corner a romantic feel.

In the wild woodland garden, a host of azaras, myrtuses and magnolias are among a variety of mature specimen plants. Nearby, the renowned rhododendron garden is the setting for many of the original Kingdon-Ward plants, and has recently been restored. From here, a path leads visitors to the river garden, where the valley floor at the base of a steeply sloping rockery, has become a wild water garden on a scale that is unmatched in Ireland. Beneath a dense canopy of gunnera leaves, colonies of lush plants jostle for space with dense groves of bamboo and massive cordylines, creating an extraordinarily exotic haven.

In December 2015, Annes Grove House and Gardens were generously donated to the state by the Annesley family. Now in the expert care of the OPW, Annes Grove is currently undergoing an ambitious programme of restoration. Together with research aimed at fully identifying its remarkable natural collection, this initiative aims to ensure the continued care and enjoyment of this rare and precious paradise.

ANNES GROVE

Annesgrove
Castletownroche
Co. Cork

General Enquiries
+353 (0) 87 251 5965
www.heritageireland.ie

DONERAILE
COURT

A remarkably intact country estate that spawned
an international horse racing tradition

COUNTY CORK

Text by:
Ellen
Brickley

Previous page
THE GEORGIAN
HOUSE AT
DONERAILE

A VIEW OF THE
WEIR

THE TRIUMPHAL
NEOCLASSICAL
GATEWAY

Doneraile Court, with its extensive walkways, water features and herds of deer, is a haven of tranquillity located close to Mallow in north Co. Cork. The landscape is laid out in 'Capability Brown' style, which is characterized by a natural, flowing appearance as opposed to more formally patterned gardens. The playground and walkways are ideal for an active family day out, and the avenues of mature trees and paved routes are perfect for a relaxing stroll under the leaves.

The House and grounds are of national significance. The estate was the home of the St Leger family for thirteen generations, until 1969. Following decades of care by the Irish Georgian Society, the property passed to the OPW in 1994. The House was largely built in the early to mid 1700s but some of its interior features date from as early as the seventeenth century, including a significant timber-panelled room. The ground floor of the House is the setting of the famous story of the 'lady Freemason'.

Elizabeth St Leger was the only daughter of Arthur, 1st Viscount Doneraile, an active Freemason who occasionally hosted Lodge meetings in his home at Doneraile Court. The exact date of this event is not known, but it is believed to have taken place between the years 1710 and 1712, prior to her marriage. Elizabeth was, at the time, in her late teens, and purportedly fell asleep in the family library one evening. She awoke to hear a clandestine Masonic ceremony taking place in the adjoining room. Elizabeth attempted to sneak out of the library, but was caught by the family butler, who was standing guard outside the room. When her father and

his friends realized that Elizabeth had overheard the secret proceedings, she was sworn in as a lodge member in order to protect the privacy of their practices. Records of Elizabeth St Leger's life are minimal, but she remained a member of the Freemasons and is seen wearing Masonic symbols in portraits. A plaque recording Elizabeth's status as the first lady Freemason was erected close to her final resting place in St Fin Barre's Cathedral in Cork city, where she is buried under her married name of Elizabeth Aldworth.

Doneraile is also an important place in the annals of horse racing, as a momentous race took place there in 1752. Two riders, Edmund Burke and Cornelius O'Callaghan, made a bet as to whose horse could cover the distance fastest between the church steeples of Buttevant and Doneraile. Their race, over a distance of four miles from steeple to steeple, took them past many natural obstacles and resulted in the term 'steeplechasing'. A horse race in which competitors are obliged to jump obstacles such as ditches and fences is still known by this term today. What is not known, however, is which of the men won their bet!

The literary credentials of the town of Doneraile are substantial, as the celebrated Irish authors Elizabeth Bowen and Canon Patrick Sheehan lived locally for much of their lives. Elizabeth Bowen is perhaps best remembered for her novel *The Last September*, which chronicled the last days of an Irish 'big house'. As well as serving as the parish priest in Doneraile, Canon Sheehan was a novelist and man of letters, and acted as an intermediary between the St Leger family and their tenants during times of political unrest.

Deeply entwined with the social and literary history of Munster and of Ireland, Doneraile is a jewel of north Cork that should not be missed.

DONERAILE COURT

Doneraile
Co. Cork

General Enquiries
+353 (0) 87 251 5965
www.heritageireland.ie

FOTA
ARBORETUM
&
GARDENS

A semi-tropical exotic garden in the waters of
Cork Harbour

COUNTY CORK

Text by:
Niamh
Guihen

Fota Arboretum and Gardens are of international significance, having one of the finest collections of rare and tender trees and shrubs grown outdoors in Europe. They are located on Fota Island, which lies in the waters of Cork Harbour, and include formal pleasure gardens, a Victorian fernery, an orangery and walled gardens, a sunken garden and a sun temple.

The name 'Fota' derives from the Irish 'fód te', meaning warm soil, and it is the site's brown earthy soils, coupled with the mildness of the local climate that have allowed many tender plants that could not be grown outdoors elsewhere in Ireland, to flourish here. The development of gardens such as Fota was stimulated by the introduction to Ireland of large numbers of exotic plant species by plant collectors working in Asia, Australia and North and South America in the eighteenth and nineteenth centuries.

Extending to 316 hectares, Fota Island was the ancestral property of the Smith-Barry family, who were descended from the Anglo-Norman warrior, Philip de Barri. Following the arrival of the Normans to Ireland in 1169 and their subsequent conquest of most of the country, Philip received large grants of lands in south Cork from King Henry II in 1177. Barryscourt, the original seat of the Barry family, was rebuilt in the fifteenth century as a fortified tower house and still stands nearby, three kilometres north-east of Fota.

In the early nineteenth century, the decision was taken by the Smith-Barry family to enlarge a modest hunting lodge that already existed on Fota Island. They engaged the services of Sir Richard Morrison, one of the foremost architects in Ireland at the time, to transform the lodge into what is now a splendid example of Regency architecture. Within the house, which forms the centrepiece of this ornamental estate, Morrison created a collection of fine Neoclassical interiors, which are still open to the public today.

By the early 1840s, James Hugh Smith-Barry had started work on the layout of the Gardens at Fota, '… beginning to convert field, wood and swamp into Arboretum, water, gardens and semi-tropical jungle'. In 1857, he was succeeded by his son, Arthur Hugh Smith-Barry, later created 1st Baron Barrymore, who continued his father's practice of planting exotic and rare trees in the grounds. In turn, his daughter, Mrs Dorothy Bell, continued this work after his death in 1925.

Today the grounds contain impressive examples of conifers from north-west America, giant redwoods, Chilean flame trees, Californian nutmegs and handkerchief trees, among many others, which thrive in the growing conditions that are particular to this part of Cork. The Smith-Barrys showed considerable sensitivity in the planting of the Arboretum as the trees are well spaced and usually planted as single specimens in a park-like setting. This generous spacing has allowed trees to grow to a large size, and means that in Fota, unlike in many other gardens and arboreta, it is possible to appreciate each individual plant and tree.

In 1975, the Fota estate was acquired by University College Cork and, in 1985, forty-seven hectares of parkland encompassing Fota House, its Arboretum and Gardens, were leased to the Fota Trust Co. Ltd. Fota's Arboretum and Gardens were later transferred to the state in January 1996, and are now under the care of the OPW. The OPW has maintained the tradition of planting exotic trees and shrubs started by James Hugh Smith-Barry over 150 years ago, thus ensuring the continued enjoyment of the grounds by the many who visit them each year.

FOTA ARBORETUM & GARDENS

Mimosa House
Fota Estate
Carrigtwohill
Co. Cork

General Enquiries
+353 (0) 21 481 2728
fota.arboretum@opw.ie
www.heritageireland.ie

ILNACULLIN / GARINISH ISLAND

An Italianate island garden in a breathtaking panoramic setting

COUNTY CORK

Text by:
Joanne
Bannon

Christopher
O'Neill

Ilnacullin is known around the world as a unique island garden of rare beauty. The Island, nestled into the sheltered coastal harbour at Glengarriff in Bantry Bay, Co. Cork has an almost sub-tropical microclimate with mild winters and high levels of rainfall and humidity. These conditions are favourable to the growth of exotic plants from many corners of the world and the Island has an internationally significant collection of rare southern-hemisphere plants. The gardens were set out in the Arts and Crafts style in Edwardian times and contain Italianate pavilions and follies, framed against a backdrop of breathtaking natural views.

Garinish Island is reached from Glengarriff village via a delightful ten-minute boat trip across the bay, which lets visitors admire a colony of seals languishing on the rocks and, with luck, catch a glimpse of the white-tailed sea eagles that nest on the Island.

Once on Ilnacullin, visitors can discover a wealth of unique architectural and horticultural gems, including a sunken Italianate garden with formal pond; the Medici pavilion, casita and lawns; walled kitchen gardens with herbaceous borders, fruit, roses and rare climbers; a Martello tower with fine panoramic views; and the Happy Valley with its Grecian temple, mature shrubberies and rare trees. The gardens have extensive collections of rare and beautiful plants including mature magnolias, rhododendrons, azaleas, leptospermums (Mānuka) and many fine southern-hemisphere trees.

Bryce House, a short walk from the walled garden, is a fitting memorial to the visionary creators and custodians of this unique place. Constructed in the 1920s in an Edwardian picturesque style, Bryce House became the residence of Violet Bryce and her son Roland, who were later joined by their housekeeper Margaret O'Sullivan and their head gardener Murdo MacKenzie.

Garinish Island has no known historical associations before the year 1800. The oldest feature of the Island today is the Martello tower, erected by the British War Office in 1805 to guard against potential Napoleonic invasion. The Island was a rocky landscape in the early 1900s, prior to its transformation into the exquisite gardens we see today.

In 1910, Garinish Island was acquired by John Annan Bryce MP, a Belfast-born merchant and Liberal politician who had worked in Burma and Siam, taking particular interest in exotic plants on his expeditions. Bryce and his wife, Violet, had been regular visitors to the area. Violet (née L'Estrange) was well acquainted with Glengarriff, having spent many childhood summers there with her cousins Countess Markievicz and Eva Gore-Booth (of Lissadell House, Co. Sligo). The Bryces commissioned Harold Ainsworth Peto, an eminent English architect and landscape designer, to design a mansion house, and to set out the gardens and their Italianate structures. In 1911, they commenced the transformation of Garinish Island to Peto's design, employing around 100 local people.

The collapse of the Russian market in 1917 brought with it the decline of the Bryces' financial fortunes, which

24

ILNACULLIN /
GARINISH ISLAND

Glengarriff
Beara Peninsula
Co. Cork

General Enquiries
+353 (0) 27 630 40
garinishisland@opw.ie
www.garinishisland.ie

prevented them from building the mansion they had originally planned. Following the death of her husband in 1923, Violet Bryce took up permanent residency in the gardener's cottage. Violet's son, Roland, joined her in 1932 and the cottage was extensively enlarged and remodelled to become an elegant middle-class home.

Bryce House and its collections were conserved by the OPW in 2015. Through original research and the use of archival and photographic material, the OPW has presented the House to reflect the period when the last owners lived there. The House is a showcase for the fascinating lives of this cultured, political family. The collection of Burmese statues, Chinese ceramics, Japanese woodblock prints, metal works and rare exotic objects reflects John Annan Bryce's adventures in Asia and his collecting interests. Old Master drawings by Salvator Rosa, Mauro Antonio Tesi and the great Venetian colourist Giambattista Tiepolo grace the walls.

The collection of antique marbles, amassed by Harold Peto for the Bryces, can be found in the House and throughout the garden. The book collection of James Bryce, British Ambassador to the United States of America, is on display in the Library. Over the years, the Bryces hosted prominent literary and cultural figures including George Russell (AE), George Bernard Shaw and Agatha Christie. Margaret O'Sullivan, the dedicated and loyal housekeeper, entertained Irish politicians, presidents, artists and writers, whose names are in the visitor book now on display in the Drawing Room. Garinish Island is a discovery point on Fáilte Ireland's

Wild Atlantic Way and welcomes some 70,000 visitors annually. The Island, which is around fifteen hectares in size, was bequeathed to the Irish people in 1953 by Roland Bryce and is cared for by the OPW. With Bryce House now restored to its former glory, careful conservation and restoration work continues on the gardens so that Garinish Island will remain a true island paradise for generations of visitors to come.

THE ENTRANCE TO BRYCE HOUSE

ONE OF TWO LARGE MARBLE URNS ON THE TERRACE

THE SPECTACULAR VIEW FROM THE ISLAND

THE GLEBE
ART
MUSEUM

An unparalleled artistic experience in Ireland's
wild north-west

COUNTY DONEGAL

Text by:
*Adrian
Kelly*

Previous page
DEREK HILL'S
STUDY

A VIEW OF THE
GLEBE HOUSE
FROM THE
GARDENS

The Glebe House and Gallery is the former home of artist and collector Derek Hill. It is perched on a hilltop that slopes down to Lough Gartan in Co. Donegal, with the Derryveagh Mountains and Glenveagh National Park serving as a spectacular backdrop. The House was originally built as the rectory to St Columba's Church, Churchill, in 1828 before being purchased by Hill in the early 1950s. Donegal is an ideal place for a landscape painter; the long northern summer days have a unique quality of light, but the weather is changeable so the artist must be quick to catch it. This suited Derek Hill's style of painting perfectly, and they were a match made in heaven.

Derek Hill was born in Southampton in 1916. He studied theatre design in Germany, France, Austria and Russia in the 1930s, but later settled on painting as a career. He was Artistic Director of the British School in Rome in the 1950s, when he bought the Glebe House. Having lived there for thirty years, Hill gave his house and its contents to the people of Ireland in the early 1980s. He was appointed a CBE in 1997 and was awarded honorary citizenship of Ireland in 1998. He died in London in 2000.

Following his arrival at the Glebe, Hill set about creating a home for himself in the wilds of Donegal that was both unique and inspiring. It is often said that every picture tells a story; in the Glebe House, everything in the collection tells a story also. The House is decorated with William Morris textiles, and impressive collections of Islamic and Oriental art. The full collection includes over 300 works by leading twentieth-century artists such as Pablo Picasso,

Edgar Degas, Pietro Annigoni and Oskar Kokoschka. In addition, there are wonderful collections of Irish and British works. At first glance, many of the objects Derek Hill collected seem completely unconnected, but together they informed his art practice and now inform visitors in a similar way. Those inspired by the Glebe have included the playwright Frank McGuinness, who used it as a source for his acclaimed play *Greta Garbo Comes to Donegal*.

In much the same way that the Glebe has been a source of inspiration for visitors, the nearby landscape of Tory Island proved to be similarly influential for Hill from the moment he first visited, soon after moving to Donegal. Tory Island is situated fourteen and a half kilometres off the Donegal coastline. Isolated and scenically stunning, it was ideal for an artist like Derek Hill, who immediately fell in love with its magnificent landscape and its people. He made the oft-perilous journey there every year to paint, staying for a fortnight. Some of his very best pictures, both landscapes and portraits, were painted on the Island.

Hill's greatest contribution to Irish art was arguably his work in fostering and promoting the Tory Island group of folk painters. The first of the Tory Island artists was James Dixon, who quickly became a world-renowned talent. The story goes that Derek Hill was painting on his first visit to Tory and Dixon, looking over his shoulder, said 'I could do better myself'. Hill challenged him, giving him paint and paper, and Dixon proved to be a wonderful, natural talent. Dixon's first painting, *West End Village*, still hangs in the Glebe House kitchen.

THE GLEBE ART MUSEUM

Churchill
Letterkenny
Co. Donegal

General Enquiries
+353 (0) 74 913 7071
glebegallery@opw.ie
www.glebegallery.ie

Spurred on by Dixon's success, other islanders began to paint and together have been creating a truly unique and comprehensive record of Tory Island life for more than sixty years now. Hill had an eye to the future, and when bringing friends and acquaintances to visit the Glebe, he always encouraged them to contribute in some way to the Donegal community. Their contributions often took the form of painting and writing. In the case of the celebrated English composer Benjamin Britten, it took the form of his magnificent work, *A Hymn for St Columba*.

The gardens at the Glebe are an artist's haven, a delightful blend of the formal and informal covering twenty acres on the banks of Lough Gartan. Hill's confidence as an artist can be seen in the garden, with its large swathes of plants and bold drifts of contrasting foliage. There are points of interest everywhere. As in all things, Hill was a collector and many of the plants came from his travels across the globe. It is no coincidence that Hill and his artist friends painted the gardens many times, and that they featured as the setting for numerous portraits. This tradition continues today at the Glebe, where it is still common to see artists at their easels in the garden, happily painting the day away.

In the early 1980s, the building used as Derek Hill's studio and guesthouse was converted into a gallery by the OPW. It now displays a series of curated exhibitions each season. The Glebe Gallery also exhibits the Derek Hill collection through a series of touring exhibitions each winter. An exciting cultural programme sees a broad range of events take place each week, with an emphasis on family activities.

An education programme runs in May and September, and throughout the winter months.

Since Derek Hill's time, the Glebe House and Gallery have been a thriving centre of artistic activity. The artworks and artefacts gathered by Hill are on permanent display in their original setting, where they continue to inform and inspire new generations of visitors. This is a museum in the true sense: a place set apart for the study of the arts; a place in which to muse, reflect and be inspired.

THE DRAWING
ROOM

THE GALLERY
IN DEREK HILL'S
FORMER STUDIO

DEREK HILL AT
THE GLEBE

33

ÁRAS AN
UACHTARÁIN

*The elegant home of Ireland's head of state in
the grandest of parkland settings*

COUNTY DUBLIN

Text by:
William
Derham

Situated on ninety-two acres within the larger expanse of Dublin's Phoenix Park, this very special estate is the official home of the President of Ireland. Having served this prestigious purpose since 1938, the house and its grounds continue to uphold a long tradition of national hospitality today.

The seeds of this tradition were sown in 1751, when one Nathaniel Clements was appointed 'Ranger and Master of the Game in the Phoenix Park'. The following year, he began work on a small red-brick home at the heart of that park, which became known as the Phoenix Lodge. In 1782, the small villa that Clements had built was sold to the Irish government of the day to provide a quiet rural retreat for the Lord Lieutenant, or Viceroy, of Ireland. From this time, it was known principally as the Viceregal Lodge but was also referred to as the Phoenix Lodge, and was used as the viceregal residence until Ireland gained its independence in 1922. From 1938, it became the home of the Irish President, acquiring the name Áras an Uachtaráin, which means 'House of the President' in Irish.

Throughout its history, the house has been both a quiet antidote to the hustle and bustle of political and city life, and a place of warmth, welcome and entertainment. Writing in 1845, Charles Lever, in his novel *Jack Hinton, the Guardsman*, described a gathering there at which 'no one seemed too old or too dignified, too high in station or too venerable from office, to join in this headlong current of conviviality'.

Previous page
THE GARDEN
FRONT

A VIEW TOWARDS
THE HOUSE IN
WINTER

The relatively modest lodge built by Nathaniel Clements has been extended many times over the centuries – for viceroys, royal guests and presidents – and these various alterations are today united behind the building's uniform, white-rendered façade. In 1951, a plasterwork ceiling from the recently demolished Mespil House, in the south of Dublin city, was rescued and later installed in the house, in what is today known as the President's Study. Depicting Jupiter presiding over the Elements and the Four Seasons, the ceiling dates from the late 1750s and has been described as 'the loveliest stucco in Ireland … the very poetry of plaster'. This superlative example of the stuccodore's art is the work of Bartholomew Cramillion, and is said to possess 'a pictorial charm which no other stuccoed ceiling in Europe can claim to surpass'. It complements one of the house's original plasterwork ceilings, also by Cramillion, which depicts episodes from Aesop's fables and is his earliest known ceiling in Ireland.

The house is most recognizable today for the vista it presents, across its gardens, when viewed from Chesterfield Avenue. At the centre of this long façade is a stately, double-height Ionic portico that presides over the formal gardens. The grounds of Áras an Uachtaráin have always been one of its chief glories. The main parterre, which forms a pair of ringed, Celtic crosses in plan, was laid out by the renowned architect Decimus Burton in conjunction with Lady Normanby, wife of the Viceroy, in 1838. It was later sketched by Queen Victoria when she stayed in the house in 1849, and today provides an elegant setting for the annual garden parties hosted by Uachtarán

ÁRAS AN UACHTARÁIN

Phoenix Park
Dublin 8

General Enquiries
+353 (0) 1 677 0095
phoenixparkvisitorcentre@opw.ie
www.president.ie

na hÉireann, the President of Ireland.

In addition to the formal parterre, the grounds contain walled gardens that have long produced fruit, vegetables and flowers for the occupants of the main house and their visitors. One of the more impressive features of the walled gardens is the Peach House. This long, linear glasshouse was designed by Richard Turner and constructed between 1836 and 1837, its purpose being, as the name suggests, to encourage the cultivation of peaches. Turner is today more famously remembered as the designer of the large palm houses at the botanical gardens in Dublin, Belfast and London. His glasshouse at Áras an Uachtaráin underwent restoration between 2007 and 2009, for which it won several conservation awards.

The grounds are also home to a daffodil garden with 140 different kinds of daffodil, and to a large number of commemorative trees, planted by many of the dignitaries and visitors who have been welcomed there over the years. Among the trees that survive today are those planted by Queen Victoria, Charles de Gaulle, John F. Kennedy, Pope John Paul II and King Juan Carlos of Spain. In recent years, these and Áras an Uachtaráin's many other delights have been enjoyed by increasing numbers of visitors through the provision of weekly guided tours. This initiative, together with the house's increasing openness to the public in recent decades, has helped make it a place with an ever-growing tradition of hospitality.

THE STATE DINING ROOM

PRESIDENT MICHAEL D. HIGGINS GREETS JOE BIDEN, JUNE 2016

THE PEACH HOUSE IN THE WALLED GARDENS

GARDENER COLLECTING APPLES

isc eatartu ag rialtas eaċtrannaċ & lér
ó mionluċt ón tromlaċ san am atá imiṫe.
ɼo dtabarfaid feidm ár n-arm an t-ionú
uan-Rialtas Náisiúnta a bunú ó ṫeaċtaí
l uile na hÉireann arna dtoġaḋ le vótaí a
ɼ & ban, déanfaid an Rialtas Sealadaċ, a
aɼ leis seo, cúrsaí sibialta & míleata na
a a riaraḋ tar ceann an pobail: Cuirimid
laċt na hÉireann faoi ċoimirce Dia Mór
cumaċt agus impímid A ḃeannaċt ar ár
arraimid gan aon duine a ḃeas ag fónaṁ
n do ṫarraingt easonóra uirti le míolao-
nnaċt ná le slad. San uair oirḃeartaċ
gas náisiún na hÉireann a ċruṫú, lena
s lena dea-iompar & le toil a clainne á
ɼ son na maiṫeasa poiblí, go dtuil
ɼó-uasal is dán di: ARNA ŚÍNIÚ TAR
is ŚEALADAIĊ, Tomás Ó Cléiriġ, Seán
ás Mac Donnċada, Pádraic Mac Piarais,
amus Ó Conġaile, Iósep Ó Pluingcéad.

ARBOUR HILL

The poignant final resting place of the leaders of Ireland's Easter Rising

COUNTY DUBLIN

Text by:
*Niamh
Guihen*

Arbour Hill is unique. Not simply a place for quiet reflection, it is a fundamental part of the foundation of the modern Irish state. The military cemetery is the last resting place of fourteen of the executed leaders of the Easter Rising of 1916.

The Cemetery has had military associations since the construction of the Royal (now Collins) Barracks in the 1700s. The oldest part of the site has been a cemetery since the 1840s, when soldiers of all ranks were buried there. The inscriptions on the headstones tell of the many countries in which the soldiers served and of the medals they received, as well as the circumstances of their deaths. Also buried in the Cemetery are local people who worked for the Barracks, as well as their families. By the late 1870s, Arbour Hill Cemetery had reached capacity and Grangegorman Military Cemetery was established nearby. Arbour Hill's connection to the 1916 Rising is what brought it from humble beginnings to a place of national importance. The Rising occurred during Easter week, taking the form of an armed insurrection against British rule in Ireland. Organized by the Irish Republican Brotherhood, those involved were members of the Irish Volunteers, Cumann na mBan, and the Irish Citizen Army. Although the Rising was not a success, the response of the British authorities to it was so severe that public support surged in favour of Irish independence.

Fourteen leaders of the Rising were tried by military court martial in Richmond Barracks and, during the first two weeks of May 1916, each of them was executed by firing squad at Kilmainham Gaol. Fearing that 'Irish sentimentality' would 'turn these graves into martyrs' shrines', General Maxwell ordered that the bodies of the leaders be taken to Arbour Hill to be buried in a single grave in the prison yard behind the military cemetery, away from public view.

In 1955, the government approved a scheme to build a large memorial at the Arbour Hill site. The design was prepared by the Assistant Architect of the OPW, Gerry McNicholl. A large screen wall was erected to separate the prison from its old yard, by then known as the 1916 Plot. Carved into the screen wall by the artist Michael Biggs was the text of the Proclamation of the Irish Republic, in both English and Irish.

On part of the prison wall that looks onto the 1916 memorial, a plaque was erected in 1966 to commemorate sixty-two other men killed during the Easter Rising. The names of the men are carved into the stone, in Irish, and the inscription at the top reads: 'Laoċra, mar aon leis na ceiṫre ċinnire ḋéag atá curṫa sa láṫair seo, a ṫug a n-anam ar son na hÉireann i 1916' ('Heroes who, with the fourteen leaders buried in this place, gave their lives for Ireland in 1916').

During his visit to Ireland in 1963, President John F. Kennedy became the first foreign head of state to honour the dead of 1916 in an official ceremony at Arbour Hill. So impressed was he by the Irish Defence Force cadets, who formed the guard of honour at the ceremony, that, for his burial a few months later, his wife Jackie requested their attendance at Arlington Cemetery.

Each May, those who died in 1916 and are buried in Arbour Hill are remembered in an official ceremony. The site today remains one of the chief memorials to the founding of the modern Irish nation.

ARBOUR HILL

Arbour Hill
Dublin 7

General Enquiries
+353 (0) 1 821 3021
superintendent.park@opw.ie
www.opwdublincommemorative.ie

DUBLIN
CASTLE

*1,000 years of history at the heart of the
nation's capital*

COUNTY DUBLIN

Text by:
Myles Campbell

From her vantage point above the ceremonial gateway to Dublin Castle, the statue of Justice gazes down on one of the most important buildings in Irish history. At first glance, the great red-brick courtyard she surveys appears to have changed little since the Georgian era. Until Irish independence, Dublin Castle was the centre of British rule in Ireland and encompassed the ceremonial palace of the country's Viceroy, who represented the British monarch. Over the years, the Castle accommodated several visiting monarchs, up until 1911, when King George V and Queen Mary made the last royal visit to Ireland before independence.

Yet if Justice were to come to life, she would surely speak not only of these echoes of the past, but also of the modern sights and sounds that are the very essence of a changed Ireland. On 16 January 1922, she witnessed the end of British rule, when Michael Collins formally took charge of the Castle on behalf of the newly independent Irish state. Today, the Castle reverberates with the fanfare of Ireland's most prestigious state ceremonies, the melodies of a lively cultural programme, and the footsteps of over a quarter of a million visitors annually, who come to form their own view of this remarkable place and its story.

That story began long before Justice assumed her current position in 1753. In 1204, King John of England gave orders for the construction of the original Castle. This fortress survived until 1684, when a fire consigned most of it to history. For visitors to the Castle today, one of its four great medieval towers, known as the Record Tower, still looms large. The only such tower still standing in Dublin, this thirteenth-century monument is a unique and precious link to a medieval city that has all but vanished.

Older still is the tenth-century stone bank that is visible in the Castle's underground excavation. Visitors who descend into this hidden cavern will see the earliest Viking feature of its type on view in Dublin. Above it is the Georgian range in which the young Bram Stoker worked before rising to fame as an author. Casting its long shadow of history all about, the adjoining Record Tower is easily imagined as a source of inspiration for Stoker's seminal novel *Dracula*.

From the ashes of the medieval Castle, a new Georgian palace arose, with the majestic State Apartments at its centre. Viceroys and British monarchs once used these elegant rooms as a backdrop to balls, banquets and grand ceremonial occasions. Since 1932, a tradition of state ceremony and entertainment has been maintained in the State Apartments by successive Irish governments. Meticulously restored and conserved by the OPW between 1964 and 1968, they remain the centrepiece of the Castle's visitor experience today. Having ascended the sweeping Battleaxe Staircase, visitors find a wealth of delicate Rococo plasterwork and a treasure trove of paintings and furniture.

Among the highlights on display in the State Drawing Room is an original portrait from 1640 by Sir Anthony van Dyck and a magnificent eighteenth-century clock by Manière of Paris. These were part of the generous Granard Bequest of 1973. At the centre of the State Apartments is the Throne

DUBLIN CASTLE

Dame Street
Dublin 2

General Enquiries
+353 (0) 1 645 8813
dublincastle@opw.ie
www.dublincastle.ie

Venue Hire & Events
+353 (0) 1 645 8800
dublincastleevents@opw.ie

Room, which features six important mythological paintings by the Italian artist Gaetano Gandolfi. In the eyes of Queen Victoria, who first used it in 1849, this great room made Dublin Castle look 'quite like a palace'. Charles Dickens took a similar view in the 1860s when he wrote of seeing 'a very glittering pageant' unfold in the space.

In contrast, the nearby room where James Connolly spent his last days, before being executed for his role in the 1916 Easter Rising, is a poignant counterpoint. Positioned just metres away from the Throne Room, it embodies the Castle's distinctive position in Irish cultural life, encompassing a heritage that is both royal and revolutionary.

The crowning glory of the Castle is St Patrick's Hall, with its spectacular painted ceiling by Vincenzo Waldré. Begun in 1788, it is the most important ceiling of its type to survive in Ireland from the eighteenth century. Over the years, many of Ireland's state visitors have been entertained beneath this magnificent feature. Since 1938, the Hall has been the setting for the nation's most significant ceremonial occasion, the inauguration of the President of Ireland. As they make their way through this space, visitors follow in the footsteps of many famous figures, from Benjamin Franklin, Nelson Mandela and Princess Grace of Monaco to John F. Kennedy, Charles de Gaulle and Queen Elizabeth II.

As well as bearing witness to many famous faces, the figure of Justice also encounters the crowds that assemble regularly for the Castle's vibrant programme of events, conferences and cultural activities. Each September, the main courtyard is transformed into an outdoor amphitheatre of music and dance for Culture Night. In the State Apartments Galleries, original exhibitions offer an engaging insight into Ireland's unique and rich cultural history, and in recent times have involved collaborations with institutions including the National Gallery of Ireland, the Victoria and Albert Museum and the Royal Collection Trust.

At Christmas, the Gothic-Revival Chapel Royal is the setting for the Castle's handmade Neapolitan crib. A captivating confection of plaster ornament and jewel-like glass, the Chapel is one of the outstanding architectural highlights of Georgian Ireland and is used throughout the year for concerts, plays and recitals.

Complementing this rich cultural offering are the Coach House Gallery, the Garda Museum, the Revenue Museum, the Hibernia Conference Centre, and the tranquil Dubh Linn Gardens, which are an invigorating oasis in the centre of a bustling city. Overlooking the Gardens is the Chester Beatty Library, which houses artistic treasures of the great cultures and religions of the world. It counts the 'European Museum of the Year' award among its accolades.

With its dynamic schedule of events and its roll call of famous figures that gets ever longer, Dublin Castle is not just a place where history was once made. Under the watchful gaze of the figure of Justice, it continues to be a vital focus of national prestige, pride and patrimony, where history is still in the making.

THE NAVE OF THE
CHAPEL ROYAL

INSTALLING
AN EXHIBITION
IN THE STATE
APARTMENTS
GALLERIES

CULTURE NIGHT AT
THE CASTLE

FARMLEIGH

The home of state hospitality with a
distinguished Guinness heritage

COUNTY DUBLIN

Text by:
Mary
Heffernan

Previous page
THE DINING ROOM

THE MAIN
ENTRANCE

Farmleigh, the delightful official residence for guests of the Irish state, occupies a site of just over seventy-eight acres contiguous to Dublin's Phoenix Park. The House and grounds were purchased by the Irish government from the Guinness family in 1999, having been in their ownership for 126 years. Farmleigh was originally purchased in 1873 by Edward Cecil Guinness, 1st Earl of Iveagh, the great-grandson of the world-famous brewer Arthur Guinness. He hired the architect James Franklin Fuller to renovate his new home, which was more than doubled in size.

Further works followed. In 1896, the architect William Young added a ballroom to the east side of the House. To this ballroom, a conservatory was added in 1901. When Farmleigh was acquired by the Irish government for use as a state guest house and conferencing facility, the OPW carefully undertook a programme of conservation of the House and grounds before opening them to visitors in July 2001.

The collections on display throughout the House today comprise works in the ownership of the OPW, together with works on loan from the Guinness family and various institutions. It is this eclectic mix that lends Farmleigh so much of its great charm.

Several of the rooms in the House retain the character of the 1st Earl of Iveagh's time, including the Billiards Room and the first-floor bedrooms. Connemara marble columns dominate the Entrance Hall. The Dining Room panelling, designed by decorators Charles Mellier & Co., incorporates four rare, late seventeenth-century Italian embroideries

once in the collection of Queen Maria Christina of Spain. A pair of cut-glass Waterford chandeliers in the corridor are scaled-down replicas of those presented by the 3rd Earl and Countess of Iveagh to Westminster Abbey, on the occasion of its 900th anniversary in the 1960s.

Among the highlights of the collection is a sculpture of Andromeda by Pietro Magni. In addition, there are a number of notable paintings, including *Stag at Bay* by Sir Edwin Landseer, *The Idle Girl* by Sir William Orpen and *The Installation of the Prince of Wales as a Knight of St Patrick* by Michael Angelo Hayes.

In one of the former drawing rooms of the House, a 'Nobel Room' has been created to honour the memory and legacy of Ireland's four Nobel Laureates for literature – George Bernard Shaw, William Butler Yeats, Samuel Beckett and Seamus Heaney.

On the second floor, the OPW has created a modern suite of rooms for state guests. The decoration of these was inspired by the designs of Ireland's singular modernist Eileen Gray. Licensed pieces from her designs, including the world-famous *Brick Screen*, *Black Board* rug and *Transat* chairs, are displayed together with editioned works by Mariano Fortuny, Andrée Putman and Jacques Henri Lartigue. These sit alongside a collection of modern and contemporary Irish and international works of art and design from the State Art Collection.

In 2009, the present Earl of Iveagh and his siblings donated

FARMLEIGH

Phoenix Park
Dublin

General Enquiries
+353 (0) 1 815 5900
farmleighinfo@opw.ie
www.farmleigh.ie

the Benjamin Iveagh Library to Dublin's Marsh's Library for permanent display at Farmleigh. The Library had been collected by the 3rd Earl at Farmleigh. It comprises some of the finest eighteenth-century Irish bindings together with important modern Irish examples, as well as a significant collection of rare first editions by Irish writers from Jonathan Swift to Seamus Heaney. Manuscript items include a thirteenth-century topographical description of Ireland, and letters written by Daniel O'Connell and Roger Casement. Scholars can access material from the collection by arrangement.

For many visitors to Farmleigh, the gardens provide enjoyment on a more regular basis. They impart a beauty, tranquillity and serenity that the OPW has determinedly maintained, aiming to conserve their historic character with minimum change. The gardens were designed and enhanced by successive generations of the Guinness family, culminating in the contributions of the late Miranda Iveagh and the landscape designer Lanning Roper. One of the most striking features of the grounds is the ornamental clock tower, which stands tall among the mature trees. Others include the large classical fountain in the Pleasure Grounds, an ornamental dairy, a garden temple, a four-acre walled garden and a sunken garden. The grounds are also home to a small herd of Kerry Black cattle, as well as donkeys and retired horses.

Several of the farmyard buildings have been converted to new uses. One is now Farmleigh Gallery, dedicated to showcasing the best of contemporary art. Another has become a theatre, while a picturesque courtyard is the location for additional state accommodation. On the site of the original boathouse, the Boathouse Café occupies a coveted spot overlooking the lake.

Since its acquisition by the state, an extensive list of distinguished guests have stayed at Farmleigh. They have included Their Royal Highnesses the Emperor and Empress of Japan, Chinese Premier Zhu Rongji and Her Majesty Queen Elizabeth II of the United Kingdom. Farmleigh also played a significant diplomatic role during Ireland's Presidency of the European Council. It was the place where the Irish government marked the formal expansion of the European Union, on 1 May 2004. Twenty-eight heads of state were present that day, when the Union embraced ten additional countries.

Today Farmleigh is synonymous with excellence in terms of the hospitality offered to guests of the nation. This excellence extends to the custodianship of this historic house, its collection and gardens. The secret of Farmleigh's success as a cultural resource has been a skilled and dedicated team. This team provides tours of the House and collections as well as education and outreach programmes, and a calendar of cultural events each year. Cared for today by the OPW, Farmleigh is a significant addition to the cultural landscape of Dublin.

GRANGEGORMAN MILITARY CEMETERY

A solemn military resting place on the fringes of the Phoenix Park

COUNTY DUBLIN

Text by:
Niamh
Guihen

Grangegorman Military Cemetery is one of the largest military cemeteries in Ireland. It was opened in 1876 to serve as a graveyard for the soldiers of the nearby Marlborough (now McKee) Barracks and their families. The Cemetery contains the remains of soldiers from across what was then the British Empire, who died naturally or were killed in action in Ireland. The graves reflect the geographical reach of British influence prior to 1922, and specific plots were laid out for soldiers from Canada, New Zealand and Australia.

Its design is that of a 'garden cemetery', a style that was promoted by J. C. Loudon, the Victorian botanist and garden designer, and became popular in the nineteenth century. The Victorians saw cemeteries not only as places where memory and status could be eternally marked in stone or marble, but also as places to visit, reflect and contemplate in a pleasant and peaceful environment. In Grangegorman, mature trees and well-maintained lawns create such a suitably reflective atmosphere amid attractive surroundings.

In total, there are over 1,100 graves at Grangegorman, including over 600 military burials and a memorial to an unknown soldier. Many of the headstones are marked with a battalion badge along with the name of the person buried beneath, their rank and date of death.

Notable graves include that of Company Sergeant-Major Martin Doyle, who hailed from New Ross, Co. Wexford. He is the only person buried in the Cemetery to have been awarded the Victoria Cross, which is the highest award for gallantry in combat in the British armed forces. Following his time in the British army, however, he joined the Old IRA in the fight against Britain for Irish independence and, later, spent more than fifteen years in the Irish army. On retiring from the Irish army, he took up a job at the Guinness Brewery and died of polio in 1940, aged 46. Significantly, he chose to be buried in his First World War uniform in the Grangegorman Cemetery despite the fact that he had spent much more of his life in the Irish army.

Approximately 16,000 soldiers serving in the regiments of the British and Dominion armies fought in Dublin during the Easter Rising of 1916. Over 130 of these men were killed in the rebellion, or later died of wounds sustained during that week. Of these, more than seventy are buried at Grangegorman. The Cemetery also holds the graves of over 140 soldiers and sailors who drowned when the R.M.S. Leinster was torpedoed by a German U-boat off the coast of Dublin on 10 October 1918.

Over 120 soldiers who died while serving with the British army in Ireland following the end of the First World War, are also buried at Grangegorman. Some of these men were killed during the Irish War of Independence, which lasted from January 1919 until a truce was called in July 1921.

Today, all of the graves are maintained by the OPW to the standards followed by the Commonwealth War Graves Commission. As is their policy, a standard red floribunda rose is planted immediately at the base of each grave.

Grangegorman Military Cemetery is today a reminder of the complicated loyalties and emotions of those who fought in the British armed forces prior to 1922, as illustrated most notably by the story of Martin Doyle. Although largely forgotten by history, they are still remembered today in this quiet and dignified corner of Dublin.

GRANGEGORMAN MILITARY CEMETERY

Blackhorse Avenue
Dublin 7

General Enquiries
+353 (0) 1 821 3021
superintendent.park@opw.ie
www.opwdublincommemorative.ie

IRISH NATIONAL WAR MEMORIAL GARDENS

A symbolic, all-Ireland monument to the fallen
of the First World War

COUNTY DUBLIN

Text by:
Niamh
Guihen

Previous page
THE CLASSICAL-
STYLE PAVILIONS BY
LUTYENS

A VIEW FROM ONE
OF THE PAVILIONS

The Irish National War Memorial Gardens at Islandbridge, Dublin, are dedicated to the memory of the 49,400 Irish soldiers who gave their lives in the Great War from 1914 to 1918. The Gardens were designed by the renowned architect Sir Edwin Lutyens and were to become his best-known public work in Ireland. They are recognized internationally as a significant example of memorial landscape architecture.

Work began on the Gardens in 1931 with the stipulation that the labour be divided, with fifty per cent coming from ex-soldiers of the British army, and fifty per cent from ex-soldiers of the Irish army. In this way, it was a truly co-operative and cross-border project, meant to commemorate the dead of the whole island of Ireland. The Gardens are a highly accomplished exercise in classical symmetry and formality, featuring tree avenues, herbaceous borders and sunken rose gardens. Eight holly trees originally stood as 'generals' on the North Terrace overlooking ranks of flowering cherry trees or 'foot soldiers'. The formality of those lines of trees contrasts boldly with the informality of the parkland trees beyond, which were chosen to provide variety and colour, seasonal interest and contrasting form.

Four 'bookrooms' in the form of classical pavilions, which represent the four provinces of Ireland, house a collection of items relating to both world wars, although there is a particular emphasis on the First World War. The best-known item in this collection is the Ginchy Cross, a wooden cross of Celtic design erected in France in 1917. The Cross served as a memorial to the 4,354 men of the 16th (Irish) Division who died in two engagements at Guillemont and Ginchy during the Battle of the Somme, in 1916. The Ginchy Cross was brought to Ireland in 1926 and was replaced in France by a stone version. Other items in the collection include Christmas cards from soldiers at the front, uniforms, passes and medals.

The approach taken to the commemoration of war dead after the First World War was very different to that of the past. The sheer magnitude of loss, and the involvement of men and women from all classes and all localities, created a need for acts of individual memorialization on an unprecedented scale. This is reflected in the memorial record books housed in one of the 'bookrooms' at the Gardens, which list the names, regiments and places of birth of the Irish soldiers known to have died in the First World War. The books are kept in cases designed especially for them by Lutyens and feature illustrations by the Irish stained-glass artist and illustrator Harry Clarke. Clarke's poignant images of soldiers on the battlefield, who appear as solitary silhouettes in the midst of swirling vine motifs, capture the impending sense of tragedy as the landscape closes in on them.

Among those commemorated in the War Memorial Gardens is Private John Condon, believed to be one of the youngest soldiers to have died in the Great War. Having lied about his age in order to join the army, fourteen-year-old Condon was killed during the Second Battle of Ypres. He is buried in Poelcapelle Cemetery in Belgium.

IRISH NATIONAL WAR
MEMORIAL GARDENS

Islandbridge
Dublin 8

General Enquiries
+353 (0) 1 475 7816
parkmanager@opw.ie
www.opwdublincommemorative.ie

At the centre of the Gardens lies the War Stone, or the Stone of Remembrance. An identical stone is found in almost all of the cemeteries of the Commonwealth War Graves Commission. In his design, Lutyens specified that 'each stone shall bear in indelible lettering, some fine thought or words of sacred dedication'. For this reason, the War Stone at Islandbridge, like so many war stones in so many cemeteries, bears the words of Rudyard Kipling, 'Their name liveth for evermore'. The War Stone is flanked by broad fountain basins, with obelisks at their centres. The impetus behind the War Stone and its engraving was to provide a sense of unity among people of different religions and traditions. As the focus of recent state commemorations that have brought together representatives of different traditions across the island of Ireland, the Gardens, which are open daily to all visitors and offer guided tours, now reflect perhaps more than ever this inclusive spirit.

THE GINCHY
CROSS

ONE OF THE
MEMORIAL
RECORD BOOKS
ILLUSTRATED BY
HARRY CLARKE

A VIEW OF THE
SLENDER GRANITE
CROSS AT THE
HIGHEST POINT OF
THE GARDENS

A VIEW ACROSS
THE GEOMETRIC
PLANTING

65

NATIONAL
BOTANIC
GARDENS
OF
IRELAND

A living national collection shaped by a heritage
of scientific study

COUNTY DUBLIN

Text by:
Matthew
Jebb

The National Botanic Gardens at Glasnevin, Dublin, have a long and distinguished history as public gardens working in botany, science, horticulture and education. Established in 1795 by the (Royal) Dublin Society, the role of the Gardens was to advance the scientific understanding of horticulture and botanical science in Ireland. Today the collections include more than 17,000 different species and cultivated forms – one of the more diverse plant collections in the world.

In their early years, the Gardens displayed plants that were useful for food, medicine and dyeing. Order beds were laid out to show an understanding of plant classification. Walter Wade, a midwife and botanist, who had petitioned parliament for the funds to establish the Gardens, delivered enormously popular lectures in botany in the early years of the nineteenth century. Ninian Niven, who was appointed curator in 1834, had formerly been head gardener at the Chief Secretary's Lodge in the Phoenix Park (now the residence of the American Ambassador to Ireland). Niven laid out the main system of paths and some of the garden features that are still present today, including the striking circular pergola known as the 'chaintent'.

It was Niven's successor in 1838, David Moore, who developed the remarkable range of glasshouses. The spectacular Curvilinear Range, designed and largely built by Richard Turner between 1843 and 1869, is of particular note. Turner was one of the leading ironsmiths of his day and his glasshouses are found across the island of Ireland, including at the Belfast Botanic Gardens.

Prominent examples of his work can also be seen at the Royal Botanic Gardens, Kew. The Curvilinear Range was faithfully restored by the OPW in 1995. Today it ranks as one of the best-preserved wrought-iron glasshouses in the world, a magnificent testament to Irish innovation and engineering.

David Moore's contribution to the Gardens, to their plant collections and to their reputation, both nationally and internationally, is unsurpassed. He also used the great interest in plants that existed among the owners of large gardens in Ireland to foster the collections at Kilmacurragh, Co. Wicklow, Headfort, Co. Meath and Fota, Co. Cork, among others. He was succeeded by his son Frederick William, who was made curator in 1879 at the age of twenty-two. Some of the gardening establishment figures of the day were sceptical that such a young man would be up to the job. Frederick William Moore soon justified his appointment and went on to establish Glasnevin as one of the great gardens of the world. In due course, he was knighted for his services to horticulture during the visit to Ireland of King George V in 1911. By the time he retired in 1922, father and son had run the Gardens for a total of over 83 years.

The scientific purposes of the Gardens were overshadowed by their horticultural reputation during Frederick William Moore's term of office. The Scientific Superintendent of the Gardens, William Ramsay McNab, had died in 1889 and had not been replaced. This hiatus lasted until the appointment of a plant taxonomist in 1968 and

NATIONAL BOTANIC
GARDENS OF IRELAND

Glasnevin
Dublin 9

General Enquiries
+353 (0) 1 804 0300
botanicgardens@opw.ie
www.botanicgardens.ie

the transfer of the National Herbarium, along with its scientific staff, from the National Museum, in 1970.

Since their foundation, the mission of the Gardens has gradually shifted. In their early years, the Gardens demonstrated plants for their utility, medicinal properties and biological relationships. Today they are an important repository for some of the world's most endangered plants, as well as a centre for research on Irish and world flora through the National Herbarium. The Herbarium holds a collection of over half a million dried plant specimens, a museum of economic botany, and a state-of-the-art DNA laboratory, complemented by an extensive research library.

Exhibitions, concerts, lectures and horticultural training days, as well as events and activities for children, make the Gardens a centre for the arts as well as sciences. The Gardens hold one of the largest collections of botanical art in the state and each September and October, the annual Sculpture in Context exhibition provides a fresh perspective as over 100 sculptural pieces enliven the grounds, glasshouses and exhibition gallery.

These important Gardens have a long history as a centre of excellence in horticulture and as Ireland's leading horticultural institution. The Gardens provide leadership and support for gardening and horticulture in Ireland, not only by demonstrating best practices but also by working closely with horticultural societies and other bodies. Indeed, many of Ireland's great gardeners undertook their initial training at Glasnevin.

The sixteen hectares of grounds comprise an extensive arboretum with large collections of oak, yew, walnut, pine, birch, beech, rowan, holly, ash and lime. A range of other garden features include a native area displaying Irish plant habitats, order beds, a rockery, herbaceous border, alpine house, rose garden and woodland garden. Extensive peat beds also allow a modest collection of rhododendrons on what is otherwise a strongly alkaline soil. An organic vegetable garden has been established that showcases methods of cultivating soft fruit, and of composting. There is even an apiary where bees can be viewed safely through a glass screen. Large collections of irises, chrysanthemums, dahlias, peonies, buddleias and tender climbers provide inspiration to gardeners. There are also biogeographic collections of plants from China, New Zealand and South Africa, besides extensive shrubberies of plants from around the world.

The Gardens work both in Ireland and around the world, in protecting and furthering the understanding of plant diversity through programmes in horticulture, scientific research, environmental education and conservation, as well as providing visitors with a beautiful place for relaxation. The Teagasc College of Amenity Horticulture is based at the Gardens, and 300 students a year have the opportunity to interact with the extensive, labelled collections. It is the complex interaction between these diverse roles and activities that makes the National Botanic Gardens unique.

THE CURVILINEAR RANGE

ONE OF MORE THAN 17,000 DIFFERENT SPECIES CULTIVATED IN THE GARDENS

CHILDREN AT PLAY

71

RATHFARNHAM
CASTLE

A palimpsest charting aristocratic taste from
Elizabethan to Georgian times

COUNTY DUBLIN

Text by:
Eoin
O'Flynn

Catherine
O'Connor

For more than 400 years, Rathfarnham Castle has been a prominent landmark in south Dublin, serving variously as a formidable private fortress, a stylish Georgian mansion and an austere Jesuit residence. In state care for the past thirty years, the Castle today welcomes visitors who wish to explore and learn about its rich and varied history.

Rathfarnham Castle was built as a fortified house during the reign of Queen Elizabeth I, serving as a private residence for one of the most powerful politicians and clergymen in late sixteenth-century Ireland, Adam Loftus. A Yorkshire clergyman, Loftus arrived in Ireland in 1560 and went on to become Archbishop of Dublin and, later, Lord Chancellor of Ireland. The house he constructed was radically modern for the time and was heavily influenced by new ideas about defensive architecture from Continental Europe. While it was also a home of comfort and luxury befitting the status of its wealthy owner, its angled corner towers, each equipped with a series of musket loops, allowed a garrison of soldiers to defend the building when necessary. These features hint at the violent and troubled context in which Rathfarnham Castle was built.

Adam Loftus had arrived in an Ireland engulfed in the political and religious upheavals sparked by the Reformation and he commissioned a building that would afford him some protection from his hostile Irish neighbours, the O'Byrnes and O'Tooles, who dwelled in the mountains to the south. The building saw military action in the seventeenth century, during the Irish Confederate Wars and the later Cromwellian Wars, and it served as a refuge for the extended Loftus family and their allies when much of the country rose in rebellion.

Visitors to Rathfarnham Castle today learn about these troubled beginnings but what they see is largely the product of a later, more peaceful age. The interior of the house built by Adam Loftus was extensively remodelled and redecorated by a series of later owners, particularly during the eighteenth century, when it was transformed into a delightful villa with richly decorated interiors for use as a place of entertainment and display. It is these exquisite interiors that largely characterize the building today.

Perhaps the most notable of the later works are those commissioned by Henry Loftus, a distant descendant of the first owner. He employed the eminent architect Sir William Chambers to design several rooms, including the Gallery. The house was transformed from an old-fashioned, semi-fortified structure into the fashionable eighteenth-century country mansion that became known as Rathfarnham Castle. Chambers famously designed Somerset House in London as well as the Casino at Marino, Charlemont House (now the Hugh Lane Gallery) and the Chapel at Trinity College, all in Dublin.

Another hugely influential designer, James 'Athenian' Stuart, was employed about the same time to produce designs for several of the Castle's Greek Revival interiors. The Saloon, the Four Seasons Room and the Gilt Room are attributed to him. Together, these contrasting works by Stuart and Chambers, two of the defining figures in

RATHFARNHAM CASTLE

Rathfarnham
Dublin 14

General Enquiries
+353 (0) 1 493 9462
rathfarnhamcastle@opw.ie
www.rathfarnhamcastle.ie

the revival of Greek and Roman classicism respectively, evoke something of the diverse nature of Neoclassical architecture in the period and are important examples of Ireland's Georgian heritage.

The Loftus family sold Rathfarnham Castle in the mid-nineteenth century and it was occupied by a prosperous professional family, the Blackburnes, who lived there until 1911. Following their departure, the Castle was bought by the Society of Jesus and was used as a house of studies, where trainee Jesuit priests were accommodated while attending college in the city, and as a retreat house, where lay groups came for contemplation and prayer. A collection of photographs from that time show how the Castle was transformed. Among the most significant interventions was the conversion of the Gallery for use as a chapel.

Following the departure of the Jesuits and the sale of the Castle and its lands to developers in 1986, the fate of this historic building was uncertain. Later that year, it was declared a national monument and in 1987 it was purchased for the nation. Since that time, an extensive programme of conservation and restoration has secured the historic fabric of the building, while work continues on returning the principal Georgian interiors to their former glory. A collection of fine original paintings, both landscapes and portraits, help to explain the story of the now vanished demesne landscape that once surrounded the Castle, as well as illustrating key personalities in the history of Rathfarnham. One of the highlights is a portrait of Lady Lucy Loftus, which is attributed to Sir Peter Lely, court painter to King Charles II.

In 2014, during construction work, an exciting archaeological discovery was made at Rathfarnham Castle, which yielded 17,500 artefacts dating from the end of the seventeenth century. The haul emerged from an old wash pit that had been blocked up, in an area beneath one of the corner towers. This discovery has shed important new light on the lifestyle of Rathfarnham's inhabitants at that time and has added more narrative threads to the already fascinating fabric of one of Dublin's most intriguing historic sites.

THE LAYERS
OF DIFFERENT
CENTURIES
REVEALED

THE GALLERY

THE CEILING OF
THE GILT ROOM

ST ENDA'S PARK & THE PEARSE MUSEUM

A home that inspired an artistic family and
sparked an Irish cultural revolution

COUNTY DUBLIN

Text by:
*Matthew
Jebb*

The significance of the house and grounds at St Enda's in Rathfarnham, Dublin, is largely due to its having been home to Patrick Pearse. As one of the seven signatories of the Proclamation of the Irish Republic, Pearse was executed for his role in leading the Easter Rising of 1916. It was in 1910, while on an historical pilgrimage of sites associated with the revolutionary Robert Emmet, that Pearse had first come upon the building known then as 'The Hermitage' in Rathfarnham. This was a seminal moment not just for Pearse but also for St Enda's School and, in a broader sense, for the history of the Irish Republic.

In 1908, Pearse had founded his bilingual school, Scoil Éanna, in Cullenswood House, Ranelagh. His initial interest in education stemmed from his involvement in the Gaelic League and the Irish language movement. He quickly became passionate about education and its possibilities. Pearse sought to challenge what many perceived as an Irish education system designed to serve the political interests of Britain, aiming instead to emphasize the virtues of Ireland's heroic past and instil pride in its language and arts. For Pearse, the key to real learning was inspiration, and he felt that if his school were to achieve success, it would require a suitably inspiring setting. When he saw the Hermitage, he realized its dual potential to provide his pupils with access to the natural world as well as to a remarkable built landscape of Norse/Celtic follies celebrating Ireland's mythological past.

The estate's first name had been the 'Fields of Odin', and was later changed in the mid-nineteenth century to 'The Hermitage' by the Hudson family, who built the house and follies. St Enda's School moved to the site in 1910 and, over time, lent its name to the park that surrounds it. Senator Margaret Pearse bequeathed the house and its contents to the state in 1968 to be used as a memorial to both of her brothers, Patrick and William. The Museum opened in 1979 and the house has undergone major renovations since.

The Museum is dedicated to both Pearse brothers. In comparison to his famous brother, William has often been an overlooked figure, and his output as a sculptor is largely forgotten. A gallery in the Museum has been devoted exclusively to his work. It includes items from the collections of Kilmainham Gaol Museum, the National Museum of Ireland and private individuals. There are two permanent exhibitions; that on the ground floor explores the life and times of Patrick Pearse, while the first floor rooms have been reconstructed to give an impression of how the Pearse family lived and worked.

Visitors can encounter furniture and objects from the collection in their original context. Side by side with these rooms are the more public spaces in which Pearse's pupils lived and studied: the boys' dormitory, school museum, school art gallery and the school chapel. The aesthetic ambience of the school was important to Pearse. The school art gallery has been recreated in its original location and features works by Beatrice Elvery, Patrick Tuohy, W. B. Yeats and Count Casimir Markievicz.

ST ENDA'S PARK &
THE PEARSE MUSEUM

St Enda's Park
Grange Road
Rathfarnham
Co. Dublin

General Enquiries
+353 (0) 1 493 4208
pearsemuseum@opw.ie
www.pearsemuseum.ie

In the basement of the house, a permanent exhibition explores the life and times of Patrick Pearse. The purpose of the display is to illustrate the full diversity of Pearse as a complex and multi-faceted character. This is communicated largely through his own writings and through first-hand accounts of Pearse written by his contemporaries, rather than through the secondary commentary of others. The intimate rooms each portray a different aspect of Pearse's life and character: the Child, the Gael, the Master, the Hermit, the Rebel and, finally, the Martyr. In the adjacent walled courtyard, there is a café and a nature room, which provides young visitors with the opportunity to learn about the natural world. A classroom has also been recreated using wall charts, plaster casts and other historic materials that would have been typical of the school.

The grounds are much as they were in Pearse's day and are a rare surviving example of an eighteenth-century park within the city. The former hay meadows now host three GAA pitches. The walled garden, where vegetable-growing classes were once delivered to the pupils, is now a quiet place for visitors. A specially commissioned sculpture by Stephen Burke to mark the centenary of Pearse's death surrounds the central fountain. Each line of Pearse's last poem, 'The Wayfarer', written the night before he was executed, is engraved in a separate slab of Donegal sandstone, providing a meditative trail for visitors to follow.

Of particular interest is the unique collection of small buildings, structures and follies dotted around the landscape, which date from the late eighteenth and early nineteenth centuries. They were built by two generations of the Hudson family. These structures have been extensively restored and repaired in recent years. They were once used by the school as natural backdrops to the pageants that were performed annually at its open days. Patrick Pearse referred to these as Aeridheacht, literally 'Taking the Air'. The structures include a summerhouse; the Hermitage, with a dolmen or druid's altar in front; a series of three rustic stone arches; and a small 'star fort' known locally as Emmet's Fort. There is also the Druid's Glen, which consists of a stone seat and a portal to a tomb; a cromlech with a tall stone spire; an obelisk; and a complex building known as the Tower Stair, which spans many periods and contains a hydraulic ram. Among all of these follies is an ogham stone that quotes a line from the ancient Roman poet Horace, in Latin. Accompanied by the name 'Edward Hudson', it reads: 'The neighbours just smile as I shift my turf and stone'. It is an amusing and self-deprecating comment on Hudson's unusual collection of structures.

The history of the house and landscape at St Enda's has largely been eclipsed by the story of Patrick Pearse's life, deeds and character, but Pearse's ambition, to create an environment where many functions were combined – the aesthetic, the wild, the productive and the theatrical – still lives on there today.

THE ENTRANCE HALL

SCOIL ÉANNA CLASSROOM

CUPS AND SAUCERS USED BY PATRICK AND WILLIAM PEARSE ON THE MORNING OF THE 1916 RISING

83

ST STEPHEN'S GREEN PARK

A Victorian civic gem in Dublin's greatest
garden square

COUNTY DUBLIN

Text by:
Niamh
Guihen

St Stephen's Green, in the heart of Dublin, is Ireland's best-known Victorian public park. The Park was laid out between 1877 and 1880 and retains many of its original features, including monuments and sculptures, water features and fountains, and Victorian planting. Other notable features include a garden for the visually impaired, an elegant bandstand, a bog garden, a playground and a rockery with alpine plants.

Prior to the creation of the Park, St Stephen's Green was a marshy site used for grazing livestock. Its name originated from an eponymous church that in medieval times was once attached to a leper hospital. In 1663, it was decided by the City Assembly to change its use to a park so that 'citizens of the city and others could walk and take the open aire'. During much of the eighteenth century, the Park was considered a fashionable place to be seen, owing to the development of its surrounding Georgian townhouses and the rise of adjoining affluent thoroughfares such as Grafton Street and Dawson Street. Walks such as the 'Beaux Walk', on the northern side of the Park, were popular promenades. In 1732, Mrs Delany confidently asserted that it 'may be preferred justly to any square in London ...'

By the nineteenth century, the condition of the Park and its features had deteriorated. The perimeter wall was in disrepair and the trees were in bad condition. In 1814, the representatives of the local householders on the perimeter of the Green, or 'commissioners', were given control of the Park. They introduced the existing granite bollards around the perimeter, as well as ornate railings, which replaced the boundary wall. The commissioners also planted trees and shrubbery and added new walks. However, the Green became a private park for the residents living along its perimeter, and only those with keys had access to this secluded sanctuary.

Among the most prominent figures associated with the Green is Sir Arthur Guinness, later 1st Baron Ardilaun. Continuing a family tradition of philanthropy, and with the support of the government, he purchased it and initiated an ambitious remodelling of the grounds, following which they were handed back to the public by means of the St Stephen's Green (Dublin) Act 1877. A fine statue of him erected on the west side of the Green in 1891 commemorates this generous legacy. On 27 July 1880, without any ceremony, the gates of the Green opened to the public once again.

The layout of the remodelled Green had been planned by William Sheppard, with suggestions made by Lord Ardilaun. Since then, the Park has changed little. Trees have matured, commemorative statues have been added and indeed some have disappeared, such as the grand equestrian statue of King George II by John van Nost, which stood at the centre of the Park from 1758 until it was blown up in 1937. In 1907, the triumphal Fusiliers' Arch was erected at the north-west corner entrance to the Park, to commemorate members of the Royal Dublin Fusiliers who had died in the Second Boer War. Many of the more recent sculptures are representative of Irish

ST STEPHEN'S GREEN PARK

Dublin 2

General Enquiries
+353 (0) 1 475 7816
www.ststephensgreenpark.ie

literary figures. Among these are a bust of the poet James Clarence Mangan by Oliver Sheppard, an abstract figure of W. B. Yeats by Henry Moore and a bust of the war poet Thomas Kettle by Albert Power.

In April 1916, the Green played a significant role in the Easter Rising. Led by Countess Markievicz and Michael Mallin, over 100 Irish Citizen Army volunteers occupied the Green, digging trenches at six of the entrances and barricading the others with park furniture. British soldiers occupied the Shelbourne Hotel, which provided an excellent vantage point over the Park. With the two forces in these positions, the Green saw some of the fiercest fighting of Easter week. However, both sides observed a twice daily truce to allow James Kearney, the Park Superintendent, to feed the ducks. He was later complimented by his superiors for having 'fed the ducks in the Green daily under considerable risk of being shot'. Kearney later listed damage to the Green in a report: 'I am sorry to say that six of our water fowl were killed, seven of the seats broken and about 300 shrubs destroyed, some of the tools were missing, a constable's oil cape torn, also the roof of the pavilion and lodge much injured'.

There are over 750 trees within the Park, among them oak, birch, holly, weeping ash and hawthorn. The perimeter is heavily planted to shelter the Park from noise and air pollution. Sycamores have a long tradition in the Green, having been the first trees planted there in the seventeenth century. There is also a formal walk of lime trees along the northern boundary of the Park. In addition, the Green is home to numerous different types of birds, including goldcrests, magpies, robins and wrens. There are at least five types of birds living in St Stephen's Green Park that are increasingly vulnerable in Ireland, including the mute swan, the tufted duck and three types of gull.

At the centre of the Park is a formal area featuring twin granite fountains and Victorian flowerbeds planted with tulips, geraniums, wallflowers and petunias, among many other types of bedding plant. Just to the north of this area, the lake is one of the most prominent features of the Park, complete with waterfall and island. It provides a habitat to a host of different waterfowl, including mallard ducks, swans and moorhens, and numerous other species of birds and fish.

Over 3.5 million people pass through St Stephen's Green Park each year. Some come early in the morning to enjoy the wonderful scent of spring bedding hyacinth in the floral displays, others in the afternoon to enjoy a performance in the bandstand. Whatever their purpose and whatever the time of day, or year, for many of those who are familiar with the Green, it is indeed 'preferred justly' to any square of its kind, just as it was for Mrs Delany all those years ago.

THE PARK IN HIGH SUMMER

A BUST OF JAMES CLARENCE MANGAN BY OLIVER SHEPPARD

THE VIEW FROM THE PAVILION

89

THE CASINO
AT MARINO

An intriguing garden temple whose secrets
dazzle and delight

COUNTY DUBLIN

Text by:
John
Fitzgerald

Maria
O'Hanlon

The Casino at Marino in north Dublin is one of the finest architectural masterpieces of eighteenth-century Europe. Small in scale yet incomparable in sophistication, it was designed in about 1759 as a pleasure house for James Caulfeild, 1st Earl of Charlemont by one of the leading architects of the time, Sir William Chambers.

In 1755, Charlemont returned to Ireland after an extensive exploration of Italy, which became his adopted home. Having also ventured as far afield as Greece, Egypt and Asia Minor, he returned with a vision to recreate an Italianate paradise in Dublin and to share it with the people of Ireland. His aspiration was to invite selected guests to the Casino to discuss politics, philosophy, the arts and sciences – themes reflected in the building's stuccowork. With the skills of Chambers, whom he had met in Rome, Charlemont embarked on the creation of a building that would represent all that is ideal in Neoclassical architecture.

Together, Charlemont and Chambers created a unique and intriguing garden temple from which to take full advantage of the magnificent panorama of Dublin Bay. Rigorously symmetrical and designed to be viewed in the round, it is a celebration of the purity and consistency of ancient classical architecture: a miniature classical temple for the Age of the Enlightenment. The plan of the Casino is in the shape of a Greek cross, arranged on a base that is only fifty feet square. Passers-by would be forgiven for presuming that the temple has just one large chamber within, but this is a remarkably clever structure full of architectural tricks, devices and illusions. Hidden inside the Casino are not one but sixteen rooms, arranged over three floors.

Chambers used various tricks to alter the impression of the Casino's scale and height and to conceal its functional components within decorative features. Urns hide chimneys, balustrades screen windows, jib doors lead to concealed spaces and four of the twelve Doric columns surrounding the building are hollow to allow for drainage from the roof. Only part of the great front door actually swings open to admit visitors. The Casino, meaning 'small house', surprises visitors as they discover the remarkable secrets of this architectural gem.

On the exterior, statues of Bacchus, god of wine, and Ceres, goddess of agriculture, sit above the north-facing entrance, symbolizing the harvest and abundance. On the south front, visitors encounter Venus, goddess of love, and Apollo, god of sun and music, with their promise of a warm welcome and entertainment within. The lavishly decorated yet compact interior of the Casino displays intricate architectural motifs, richly patterned parquetry floors and beautifully executed plasterwork.

The principal floor was once used to display Charlemont's various artefacts and artworks. It is richly decorated with stucco representations of musical instruments, agricultural tools and mythological figures. The intricate floors are formed of woods imported from distant corners of the eighteenth-century British colonies. The principal apartment in the Casino is the Saloon. Its stuccowork ceiling features a representation of Apollo, whose head emerges from a

THE CASINO AT MARINO

Cherrymount Crescent
Malahide Road
Marino
Dublin 3

General Enquiries
+353 (0) 1 833 1618
casinomarino@opw.ie
www.casinomarino.ie

dazzling sunburst. The room's south-facing window frames the spectacular view over Dublin Bay and the mountains, which Charlemont frequently compared to the view across the Bay of Naples. Jib doors on either side of the Saloon lead into the Zodiac Room and the China Closet.

The winning impression created by the Casino is immediately apparent from a description of it written by Lady Shelburne in 1769: 'The curiosity of the place consists of a very fine Temple, Lord Charlemont is building at very great expense … The architecture is very correct and the stonework well executed. In the inside is a room for dining in and overlooking the fine prospect, which may contain the company of 12 or 14 people … The floors are parquetted in the most sumptuous wood, painted satin furniture, gilding and every other expense is lavish'd on ye decoration of it.'

In the Casino's basement there are several service rooms and a door leading to a series of eight underground tunnels that surround the building. These tunnels are lit from above by grilles and are one of the Casino's most intriguing components. After the estate was sold in the late nineteenth century, members of the Irish Volunteers, who rented rooms nearby, are thought to have hidden guns in the tunnels prior to the 1916 Easter Rising. During the revolutionary period that followed the Rising, the area around Marino and Fairview was a hotbed of Volunteer activity. There are even accounts of Michael Collins using the tunnels for shooting practice during the War of Independence, and training with the first two Thompson machine guns to reach Ireland.

In the 1940s, a photograph of 83 former members of the Irish Volunteers, who were part of F Company, 2nd Battalion, Dublin Brigade and who were based in the Fairview area in the early twentieth century, was taken on the south lawn of the Casino. This remarkable reunion image is a reminder of a fascinating and comparatively unknown chapter in the building's history.

Nowadays little is left of Lord Charlemont's surrounding estate apart from the great accounts of entertainment found in letters written by various guests like Lady Shelburne. A hermitage and a Gothic folly no longer survive, but the Casino, Charlemont's pride and joy, remains remarkably intact. In 1984, a decade of restoration work was completed by the OPW. The 'care and restraint' with which this painstaking work was carried out earned the project the first medal for restoration to be awarded by the Royal Institute of the Architects of Ireland. Since then, the building has experienced a new lease of life as a venue for various events, including musical recitals and exhibitions. Guided tours of the Casino are available from March to October, when tales of its glory days are re-told and the magnificence of the estate re-imagined. Regarded internationally as a cameo of exquisite craftsmanship, the Casino continues to thrive today as the legacy of Lord Charlemont's vision.

95

THE
GARDEN OF
REMEMBRANCE

A monument to Ireland's freedom, evoked
through an image of its Celtic past

COUNTY DUBLIN

Text by:
Niamh
Guihen

The Garden of Remembrance lies at the heart of the city of Dublin and is dedicated to the memory of all those who gave their lives in the cause of Irish freedom.

The site on which the Garden of Remembrance was laid out is an historic one. In the eighteenth century, it was the location of a series of pleasure gardens that were used, from 1748, to raise funds to build the first maternity, or 'lying-in', hospital in Britain and Ireland. This institution, the Rotunda Hospital, was opened in 1757 and survives today. The hospital occupies the southern side of Parnell Square, while the Garden of Remembrance today occupies a portion of what were once the pleasure gardens, to the north. In 1916, following the Easter Rising, the enclosed grounds of the Rotunda Gardens were where many of those involved in the Rising were temporarily held, before being taken to Kilmainham Gaol, where the leaders of the Rising were executed.

The site for the Garden of Remembrance was acquired by the government in 1938, but the outbreak of war the following year delayed the start of work. Eventually, in 1946, a competition was held for the design of the memorial garden.

The winner of this competition was the architect Daithí Hanly, who proposed a symbolic, cruciform design running east to west across the top of the square. The long, sunken garden he created contains a large cross-shaped pool, symbolic of the dead, decorated with a tiled mosaic. The mosaic depicts swords, shields and spears thrown beneath the waves. This is a reference to the ancient Celtic custom of casting weapons into water as a sign of peace following battle.

When the mosaic for the bottom of the pool was being designed, Dr Joseph Rafferty of the National Museum of Ireland was consulted, and suggested putting heraldic boars on one of the shields. However, when the mosaic was complete, Hanly noticed that rather than 'three fierce hairy boars with long tusks', it depicted 'three modern bacon-producing pigs'. He expressed his dismay to the artist, who replied that 'only a farmer could tell the difference!' By this stage it was too late to change the mosaic and so the pig-like boars can still be seen in the Garden today.

Hanly left the west end of the Garden empty for a commemorative sculpture. The sculptor selected for the project, Oisín Kelly, struggled to find an appropriate design, searching for something that was 'universal, simple and part of the popular imagination'. Eventually he settled on the tale of 'The Children of Lir', drawing inspiration from an old Irish legend and the poetry of W. B. Yeats. The legend tells of how the four children of the Irish king, Lir, were transformed into swans and exiled to three Irish lakes for a total of 900 years. The twenty-five-foot high sculpture is based on the idea that at certain moments in history men are transformed utterly, and compares the 900-year plight of the swan children with the Irish struggle for independence.

In 1966, on the fiftieth anniversary of the 1916 Rising, the Garden was formally opened to the public. Today many dignitaries who visit Ireland make a stop at the Garden. In 2011, on the first day of her historic state visit to Ireland, Queen Elizabeth II laid a wreath there. This was a significant gesture, one that symbolized a new era in Anglo-Irish relations. The Garden is open to everybody on a daily basis, offering a quiet space in which to stop, reflect and remember those who gave their lives in the cause of Irish independence.

THE GARDEN OF REMEMBRANCE

Parnell Square East
Dublin 1

General Enquiries
+353 (0) 1 821 3021
superintendent.park@opw.ie
www.opwdublincommemorative.ie

THE
IVEAGH
GARDENS

An enchanting secret garden offering
sanctuary in the city

COUNTY DUBLIN

Text by:
Niamh
Guihen

Previous page
THE YEW MAZE

THE RUSTIC WATER
CASCADE

The Iveagh Gardens are affectionately known as Dublin's 'Secret Garden'. Just 450 metres from St Stephen's Green and less than half the size, this Victorian park has an atmosphere that is totally unique. Tucked away behind tall buildings and surrounded by a high wall, the Gardens are peaceful and secluded. Despite being 'secret', the Gardens are enjoyed by over 430,000 visitors annually. They feature an assortment of landscape features, from formal lawns and a rosarium to a yew maze. At one end of the Gardens, at a level lower than the rest, is Ireland's first purpose-built archery ground. Many visitors to the Gardens come specifically to see the rustic water cascade, which is particularly beautiful in summer.

The Gardens were originally designed in the late 1700s by John (Jack) Scott, 1st Earl of Clonmell, as a private garden for his house on Harcourt Street. The Gardens are not the Earl's only legacy in Dublin, though, as his nickname lives on today. His red face and love of alcohol gained him the name 'Copper-Faced Jack'. In 1817, the Gardens were made public and renamed the Cobourg Gardens. For a brief period, they were a fashionable destination for Dublin's upper-class society. To mark their public opening, the newspapers reported that a 'Grand Gala and brilliant display of fireworks' was held on 18 June 1817, noting that the Gardens would be open every evening as 'a Fashionable Promenade'. By the 1830s, however, the Cobourg Gardens had declined sharply in popularity, and by the latter half of the nineteenth century were badly neglected.

In 1862, Sir Benjamin Lee Guinness co-founded the Dublin Exhibition Palace and Winter Garden Company in order to provide a public exhibition space for Irish arts and horticulture. The Exhibition Palace was built on the site of the Cobourg Gardens. In 1865 Ninian Niven, former curator of the Botanic Gardens in Dublin, designed the pleasure grounds of the Exhibition Palace. Stylistically, the design was an intermediate combination of the 'French Formal' and the 'English Landscape' traditions. One contemporary observer captured this sense of stylistic duality, describing the Gardens as having a 'geometric foreground with the mazy softness of our so called English curved lines'. Together with Niven's gardens at Hilton Park, Co. Monaghan, the Iveagh Gardens have been recognized as being 'of great importance' in terms of their design. Further examples of Niven's work can still be seen at the National Botanic Gardens and at Áras an Uachtaráin, the residence of the Irish President, but the Iveagh Gardens remain the most complete set of public gardens to have been designed by Niven in Ireland.

In 1871, Edward Cecil Guinness, later 1st Earl of Iveagh acquired the site of the Exhibition Palace and for ten years continued its tradition of public events, which included banquets, concerts and flower shows. In 1883, Guinness sold the Winter Garden structure, and a wall was built to enclose the Gardens, which once more became private. In 1939, his son Rupert Guinness, 2nd Earl of Iveagh gave them as a gift to the Irish nation. As part of this arrangement, he specified that they were never to be built upon, so that they could serve as a much-needed 'lung' for the city of Dublin.

THE IVEAGH GARDENS

Clonmel Street
Dublin 2

General Enquiries
+353 (0) 1 475 7816
www.iveaghgardens.ie

In 1991, the Iveagh Gardens were placed under the care of the OPW, and a plan was put in place immediately to undertake restoration and conservation works. Looking around the Gardens today, the fruits of this work are visible in features such as the yew maze and the delicately scented rosarium with its fine collection of roses, some of which date from before 1865. The two fountains, restored in 1994, form a magnificent centrepiece in the Gardens.

Local legend tells of an elephant buried underneath the sunken lawn at the north end of the Gardens. The story goes that while the Gardens were undergoing renovations in 1922, an elephant died in Dublin Zoo and was laid to rest under the archery grounds. However, at this time, the Iveagh Gardens were the private gardens of the adjacent Iveagh House, which faces onto St Stephen's Green. No evidence of the elephant's remains has yet been found, but the tale remains a cherished part of Dublin folklore.

The Iveagh Gardens are perhaps best known today for the many events held there during the summer. From food and lifestyle festivals to pop concerts, the Gardens remain a popular venue, maintaining their centuries-old tradition of 'brilliant display'. Yet at quieter times, as faithful visitors know and new ones will discover, they offer a sense of solitude that helps them to remain one of Dublin's best-kept secrets.

A VIEW FROM THE
ROSE GARDEN

AUTUMNAL
SOLITUDE

A VIEW TOWARDS
THE CASCADE

ONE OF THE
ORNAMENTAL
STATUES

105

THE
PHOENIX
PARK

*The vast garden playground of Ireland's
capital city*

COUNTY DUBLIN

Text by:
*Niamh
Guihen*

The Phoenix Park, encompassing over 1,752 acres at the edge of Dublin city, is one of the largest designed urban parklands in any city in the world. The Park came into being as a royal deer park created by James Butler, 1st Duke of Ormond for King Charles II, in 1662.

In the eighteenth century, it took on a decidedly military aspect. In 1710, a salute battery was erected from which cannon would fire to celebrate important public events. In 1734, the Magazine Fort was built to store gunpowder, far away from the population of the city lest the stores ignite in an explosion. Later, the Park provided a home to Mountjoy Barracks (now the office of the Ordnance Survey of Ireland), the Royal Infirmary for treating wounded soldiers and the Royal Hibernian Military School. Its open spaces also provided the location for many military displays and reviews.

In the midst of these developments, it was opened to the public by Philip, 4th Earl of Chesterfield in 1745 and became the location of residences for the Lord Lieutenant of Ireland (or Viceroy), the Chief-Secretary and the Under-Secretary. Two of these residences remain, known today as Áras an Uachtaráin, the home of the President of Ireland, and Deerfield, the home of the United States Ambassador to Ireland.

In the nineteenth century, the Park was substantially remodelled by the renowned Victorian architect and landscape designer Decimus Burton. Burton worked on the buildings and layout of the Park for more than ten years, utilizing the experience he had gained working on London's St James's Park, Green Park and Hyde Park. He produced a masterplan for Dublin's Park that included the building of new gate lodges, the strategic planting of trees and the creation and realignment of the Park's many roads, including Chesterfield Avenue. New rides and walks were created and new views opened up. The picturesque character of the Park today is largely the result of his efforts.

The Royal Dublin Zoological Society opened Dublin Zoo within the Park in 1830. The Promenade Grounds, known today as the People's Garden, opened in 1840 and were later improved in the 1860s with the addition of a head gardener's house and a rock garden.

From the 1830s onwards, and particularly after the 1860s, the Park's role as the 'lungs' of the city took on an extra dimension as sporting and recreational activities became a prominent feature of its civic life. Some of the oldest and most successful sports clubs in Ireland were formed and nurtured in its surroundings. In 1830, the Phoenix Cricket Club, Ireland's oldest, was founded in the Park; a golf course was created there in 1885; and in 1903, the Gordon Bennett Cup for auto racing was held in the Park. In the latter half of the nineteenth century, the Park came to be used more intensively for other sports such as football and hurling and, to this day, it continues to be a hub of athletic and sporting activity within the city.

Occasionally, throughout its history, the Park has also

108

THE PHOENIX PARK

Dublin 8

General Enquiries
+353 (0) 1 677 0095
phoenixparkvisitorcentre@opw.ie
www.phoenixpark.ie

been the scene of darker events. On 6 May 1882, it saw the gruesome killing of Lord Frederick Cavendish, Chief Secretary of Ireland and the Under-Secretary, Thomas Henry Burke. Cavendish and Burke were among the most senior members of the British administration in Ireland and their murder, by a republican group called the Invincibles, caused an outcry at the time.

In more recent and peaceful times, the history and landscape management of the Phoenix Park has been characterized primarily by the replanting of trees and shrubs, nearly 3,000 of which were destroyed by the great storm of 1903. The celebration of the Eucharistic Congress in 1932 and the erection of the Papal Cross in 1979 for the visit of Pope John Paul II, whose mass was attended by 1.25 million people, are just two of the many events the Park hosted in the twentieth century. Another 10,000 trees were planted as part of the management plan of 1986 and considerable arboricultural works were carried out on the mature tree population in the latter quarter of the century.

One of the highlights of the Phoenix Park today is the Victorian Walled Kitchen Garden adjoining the Phoenix Park Visitor Centre and Ashtown Castle. Beautifully restored in recent years to its original layout, the Garden is one of the Park's many places of education and inspiration for those interested in horticulture and history.

Within the Phoenix Park there are twenty-seven different habitats and six different types of woodland. For this reason, it is home to a huge variety of wildlife – of all species found in Ireland, fifty per cent of the mammals and forty per cent of the birds can be found in the Park. Most notable among the Park's many wild inhabitants is the herd of fallow deer, which is descended from that introduced by the Duke of Ormond in the 1660s.

Over the centuries, the Park has steadily evolved from a private royal hunting ground to a much-loved public amenity. Visiting it today, there is no shortage of things to see and do. The many monuments of the Park tell its story through the centuries – from the Phoenix Column, the oldest in the Park, completed on the orders of the 4th Earl of Chesterfield in 1747 to the Wellington Testimonial. These are in addition to the natural monuments that are the Park's many historic trees.

Almost 300 organized events take place every year in the Phoenix Park including runs, cycles, concerts, exhibitions, sports events, the Phoenix Park Honey Show and the Bloom garden festival. Tours today explain the history and significance of the Park, as well as giving a glimpse into the excavation within the Magazine Fort and the restoration that is still ongoing. From education to recreation, the Phoenix Park has something for everyone.

THE MAGAZINE
FORT

EXHIBITS ON VIEW
TO VISITORS

THE ROLLING
LANDSCAPE

THE
ROYAL
HOSPITAL,
KILMAINHAM

An iconic landmark on the edge of Dublin that
heralded the dawn of an Irish renaissance

COUNTY DUBLIN

Text by:
William
Derham

Previous page
THE MASTER'S
GARDENS

THE CHAPEL

This iconic building, which stands high on a prominent ridge overlooking the River Liffey, was founded by King Charles II in 1679 to accommodate the 'aged and maimed officers and soldiers' from his Irish armies. The building itself is spectacular, inspired by the famous Hôtel National des Invalides in Paris, and pre-dating by two years its sister institution at Chelsea in London. Designed by Sir William Robinson to accommodate 300 veterans of the king's wars, it has been described as 'the earliest full scale exercise of architectural classicism' in Ireland. Begun in 1680, it was occupied by its first 'pensioners' in 1684 and was largely complete by 1687.

This impressive edifice today sits at the centre of forty-eight acres of verdant landscape that was once part of Dublin's Phoenix Park. The Park can be seen on the other side of the River Liffey. To the west, an avenue extends to a Gothic-style gateway and nearby cemeteries, which have long associations with the Hospital, and with Irish history. To the north, terraces and intricate baroque gardens reinforce and enhance the axial planning and architecture of the Hospital building. Together with the western avenue, they extend the main axes of the building out into the landscape in the grand, classical tradition. Between the gardens and the cemeteries to the west lies an area known as the Meadow Fields. To the south are two ranges of stables and to the east, the Deputy Master's House. The best-known of the cemeteries is 'Bully's Acre', which dates back to before Viking times.

In Irish, 'Kil Maignenn' means Maignenn's Church, and the area of Kilmainham takes its name from that saint, who established a church and monastery here around the year AD 606. It was here, in the lands of Maignenn's Church, that two of the sons of Brian Boru, High King of Ireland, were reputedly buried in the aftermath of the Battle of Clontarf in 1014.

Following the arrival of Richard Fitzgilbert de Clare (better known as 'Strongbow') and the Anglo-Normans in Ireland, in 1169, the lands of St Maignenn's were granted to the Knights Hospitaller of St John of Jerusalem, who established a priory here. The priory continued on the site until the dissolution of the monasteries in the 1540s, but parts of its buildings remained until the 1680s, when they were likely broken down and used in the construction of the new Royal Hospital.

Integral to the original Hospital design were the baroque gardens to the north, known as the Master's Gardens. They were designed so that they could be appreciated from the terraces above, and from the Master's Lodgings that overlooked them. They were aligned with the towering steeple of the Hospital, completed in the early 1700s, and a small banqueting house that looked back towards it from the northern side of the gardens. A grand double flight of stone steps, ornamented with urns, leads from the upper terrace down to the planted walks, which form the principal elements of a classical garden – 'parterre' and 'wilderness'.

As impressive as the Hospital is within its ordered

114

THE ROYAL HOSPITAL, KILMAINHAM

Military Road
Dublin 8

General Enquiries
+353 (0) 1 612 9900
www.heritageireland.ie

Venue Hire & Events
+353 (0) 1 612 9903
info@rhk.ie
www.rhk.ie

landscape, closer examination of its interior reveals equal delights. The building is arranged around four sides of a cloistered courtyard. Three of these wings are today the home of the Irish Museum of Modern Art (IMMA) while the fourth, northern wing, contains the architectural wonders that are Robinson's Chapel and Great Hall. These two interiors are the highlights of the original building. The Chapel contains magnificent carvings in oak, armorials in stained glass and a baroque ceiling composed of a symphony of fruit, flowers, foliage and angels. The Great Hall is home to a unique collection of portraits that were painted specifically for it, most of which have hung there since at least 1713. They include paintings of King Charles II, and of James, 1st Duke of Ormond who, as Viceroy of Ireland, made the building project his own. It is his arms, and not those of the King, that adorn the building. Other treasures cared for by the OPW include the original library of the Hospital, which runs to 1,714 volumes, some dating to the 1650s.

Also in the northern wing are the Master's Lodgings. The Master of the Hospital was traditionally the commander of the army in Ireland, and so it was that after centuries of relative peace it became home to General Maxwell in 1916. While resident there, he signed the death warrants of the leaders of the 1916 Easter Rising, each of whom was executed at Kilmainham Gaol, which lies only a short walk away at the end of the western avenue.

The rebellion of 1916 heralded an abrupt change in the circumstances of the Hospital. Ireland gained its independence in 1922 and, five years later, the last pensioners departed the institution for its counterpart at Chelsea. The buildings were put to several different uses over the decades, serving as headquarters to An Garda Síochána, the Irish police force, from 1930 to 1950. To mark the 300th anniversary of the building's creation, it was comprehensively restored by the OPW between 1979 and 1984. In parallel with this, the gardens were also restored. They had become badly overgrown by the 1970s and were recreated in the spirit of the seventeenth century using original maps, the Hospital's minute books and John Evelyn's book, *Silva*, which describes the layout of an ideal garden in 1660s England.

Amid great excitement, in 1991 the Hospital became home to the new Irish Museum of Modern Art, which cares for and displays a large part of the state's contemporary art collection. Several of its larger pieces now ornament the grounds, in keeping with the spirit of an original seventeenth-century manicured landscape.

Today, managed and cared for by the OPW and home to the Irish Museum of Modern Art, the Royal Hospital at Kilmainham offers a complementary mix of calm and culture on the western edge of the city of Dublin.

RICH CARVINGS IN THE CHAPEL

THE ORNATE CEILING IN THE CHAPEL

AN ANGELIC STAINED GLASS FIGURE

DERRYNANE
HOUSE
&
GARDENS

The ancestral home of Ireland's 'Liberator'
in a stupendous coastal setting

COUNTY KERRY

Text by:
*Niamh
Guihen*

Previous page
THE DRAWING
ROOM

THE HOUSE IN ITS
MAJESTIC NATURAL
SETTING

Derrynane, which comes from the Irish meaning 'the oak wood of St Fionán', is situated on the tip of the Iveragh Peninsula, Co. Kerry. Sheltered within this woodland stands Derrynane House, the ancestral home of Daniel O'Connell – lawyer, politician and statesman, and one of the towering figures of modern Irish history.

Derrynane House was Daniel O'Connell's childhood home. Throughout his career, it was his country residence and the place where he and his family spent most of their summers. O'Connell inherited the House in 1825, and the time he spent there was one of the chief joys of his life. On 22 October 1829, he wrote: 'This is the wildest and most stupendous scenery of nature – and I enjoy residence here with the most exquisite relish … I am in truth fascinated by this spot: and did not my duty call me elsewhere, I should bury myself alive here'.

Derrynane was transferred to the state in 1964, and most of the old demesne now forms part of Derrynane National Historic Park. In 1967, the House was opened as a museum by the President of Ireland Éamon de Valera and, in 1975, the National Historic Park was formally opened by President Cearbhall Ó Dálaigh. The lands of the park are rich in natural and cultural heritage, with a unique combination of archaeological, architectural, horticultural, botanical and ecological features. These include an ogham stone, ringforts, souterrains, a Mass rock and the ruins of Ahamore Abbey.

Derrynane's cultural association with Daniel O'Connell is the principal reason for its historic importance and the House is now a museum dedicated to his life and achievements. It contains many artefacts associated with the O'Connell family, including an important family portrait collection and much original furniture.

The original, early eighteenth-century house appears to have been a two-storey building facing north. When Daniel O'Connell inherited the property from his uncle, he commenced building a two-storey, L-shaped block to the south, containing a study, dining room and stair hall on the ground floor, and a library and drawing room on the first floor. In 1844, following his release from prison, O'Connell constructed a chapel to the east of the original house, which was connected to it via a long, single-storey passage.

The House remained the home of Daniel O'Connell's descendants for more than a century. It passed first to his son Maurice and then to his grandson Daniel. His great-granddaughter, Frances, lived at Derrynane until 1958 and was the last member of the family to call it her home.

Eventually the upkeep of Derrynane became a burden on the O'Connell family and in 1947, the Derrynane Trust was founded, with the objective of preserving the House as a museum and memorial to Daniel O'Connell. The House was transferred to the Trust, which soon found the maintenance and restoration work extremely costly. Following an appeal to the government for assistance, the House was transferred to the state. By this time, much of the building, including the original, eighteenth-

DERRYNANE HOUSE

Caherdaniel
Co. Kerry

General Enquiries
+353 (0) 66 947 5113
derrynanehouse@opw.ie
www.derrynanehouse.ie

century part of the House, was in very poor structural condition. Part of the original structure was demolished and restoration work concentrated on those parts of the House built during Daniel O'Connell's ownership, which included the south wing, the library wing and the chapel. The footprint of the part of the building that was demolished is now indicated in the courtyard by a broken line of paving slabs. Restoration work was completed in 1967 and the House as seen today consists essentially of the south and east wings, built by Daniel O'Connell.

The main gardens lie to the north of the House. This area is relatively sheltered and the mild winters enable frost-sensitive trees and shrubs to thrive there. Extensive sub-tropical gardens have been developed and these include a collection of rare trees of South American origin that are endangered in the wild. The sub-tropical gardens were established as part of the National Botanical Collection. This relatively new plant collection is one of the finest in the region and includes many rare and unusual specimens.

Accessed from the House via a tunnel, the ornamental gardens encompass approximately six hectares and incorporate extensive hedging, a number of shrubberies, herbaceous beds and lawns. Enclosed by dry-stone walls, these gardens contain a significant plant collection, incorporating many young, rare and tender southern hemisphere plants. They also include bog gardens, drainage channels and irrigation features.

The National Historic Park extends to approximately one and a half kilometres of sandy and rocky shoreline, which takes in several sand dunes. The dunes and coastal area are of high ecological value and meet the European criteria for designation as Special Protection Areas and Special Areas of Conservation. The dunes contain rare animal and plant species including the natterjack toad, the narrow-mouthed whorl snail, and the Kerry lily. There are also a variety of trails throughout the grounds, including a section of the Kerry Way. Just off the shoreline is Abbey Island, which can be reached on foot across the sand when the tide is low.

Encompassing both history and horticulture, the historic property of Derrynane is a quiet delight. Whether to learn the story of Daniel O'Connell and his family or to enjoy the grounds and walks in this mild oasis on Ireland's Iveragh Peninsula, Derrynane always proves a rewarding visit.

A CORNER OF THE
DRAWING ROOM

AN AERIAL VIEW
OF THE SANDY
SHORELINE

THE DINING ROOM

123

THE GREAT BLASKET ISLAND & VISITOR CENTRE

The story of an enduring literary heritage
fostered by a unique island community

COUNTY KERRY

Text by:
Doncha Ó'Conchúir

Previous page
THE ISLAND BATHED
IN GOLDEN LIGHT

ONE OF THE
RESTORED
COTTAGES ON
THE ISLAND

AN EXHIBITION
IN THE VISITOR
CENTRE

The Great Blasket Island, Dún Chaoin, Co. Kerry, a Signature Discovery Point on the Wild Atlantic Way, remains a monument to one of the most unique communities in Irish history. Abandoned by its last permanent residents in 1953, the Island is a place of wild beauty and deep peace. On quiet days, visitors may see Ireland's largest colony of grey seals resting on An Trá Bán (the White Strand). The Island and the Visitor Centre each enjoy stunning views of the surrounding seascape. Inishtooskert, the most northerly of the six islands collectively known as the Blaskets, is nicknamed An Fear Marbh (the Dead Man) or the Sleeping Giant because of its distinctive shape when seen from the east. This quirk can be best appreciated from the famous Slea Head Drive.

The Great Blasket was inhabited continuously for at least 300 years – even during the Great Famine of the 1840s, when fishing sustained the islanders after the failure of the potato crop and not a single death was recorded from hunger. At its peak, the population reached 160, but declined to twenty-seven by the 1950s due to emigration.

During the winter of 1947, Seán Ó Cearnaigh, a young man living on the Island, became seriously ill. Due to a violent storm, neither a doctor nor a priest could access the Island before he died. Only the lifeboat from Valentia, reaching the Island three days after his death, could bring him ashore to be buried with his family. The islanders petitioned the Irish government to rehouse them elsewhere, as their safety was at risk if they remained in their homes. Following their evacuation to the mainland six years later, the village on the sheltered side of the Great Blasket fell into ruin.

Two of the Island's houses have recently been restored by the OPW, with assistance from Fáilte Ireland. One of these houses belonged to the celebrated Blasket Island memoirist Tomás Ó Criomhthain. Fitted out with simple period furniture, the restored house offers visitors a chance to walk in the footsteps of one of Ireland's most significant writers and to re-imagine the harsh vernacular living conditions endured by Tomás Ó Criomhthain and his contemporaries.

Until their relocation, the islanders survived by raising sheep, subsistence farming, fishing, and trading with the mainland, which they reached in small boats called 'naomhóga'. In spite of their light construction, these boats could carry over half a ton of material across Blasket Sound. An example of a 'naomhóg' can be seen in the Visitor Centre.

The Great Blasket Island is perhaps best known for its literary tradition, from Tomás Ó Criomhthain and Muiris Ó Súilleabháin to the legendary Peig Sayers. The islanders' use of the Irish language and their intimate knowledge of folklore attracted scholars from all over Europe in the early twentieth century. As well as her memoir, Peig Sayers contributed to the work of the Irish Folklore Commission.

The Island is open to visitors from April to late-September each year, and a guide service is available for walking tours. Access to the Island is via privately operated passenger boats, weather permitting. The Visitor Centre in Dún Chaoin, on the mainland, is open from mid-March until late-October. Along with artworks encapsulating a sense of the Blasket experience, the Centre features an audio-visual introduction to island life, a bookshop, a café, and a 'seal cam', which streams live views of the Centre's maritime neighbours. The permanent exhibition covers daily life, traditional fishing and farming methods, the Irish language and Blasket literature, and the effect of emigration on the Blasket community. The Centre is also the hub of an extensive archive of Blasket-related material, and research into the Island's history of kings and chieftains, shipwrecks and storytellers, will continue as long as the Island has secrets to tell.

THE GREAT BLASKET ISLAND & VISITOR CENTRE

Dún Chaoin
Dingle
Co. Kerry

General Enquiries
+353 (0) 66 915 6444
blascaod@opw.ie
www.blasket.ie

CASTLETOWN

A monument to the fine and decorative arts of
Georgian Ireland's golden age

COUNTY KILDARE

Text by:
Dorothea
Depner

Built in the 1720s for William Conolly, Speaker of the Irish House of Commons, Castletown was meant to exemplify its owner's influence and immense wealth. His was Ireland's first mansion built in the Palladian style, and Castletown soon became synonymous with architectural excellence, fine style and lavish entertaining that rivalled the Viceregal Court in Dublin. Over the past three centuries, visitors from all over the world have marvelled at the splendour of the house and have been enchanted by its beautiful natural setting.

The façade of Castletown House was based on designs by Florentine architect Alessandro Galilei, while the execution of the interior, the wings and colonnades fell to the young Irish architect Edward Lovett Pearce, who later designed the Irish Houses of Parliament on Dublin's College Green. Much of the interior decoration, however, remained unfinished until the second heir of Castletown, Thomas Conolly, settled there in 1759 with his young wife, Lady Louisa. The daughter of Charles Lennox, 2nd Duke of Richmond, she brought with her the style and refinement she had been accustomed to at her childhood homes in Goodwood, Richmond House and Carton, and set about modernizing her new home to suit her tastes.

The transformation Castletown underwent in the 1760s and 1770s included the installation of the magnificent cantilevered staircase under the direction of Simon Vierpyl, and the opulent stucco decoration in the Staircase Hall by the talented Swiss Lafranchini brothers. Room functions and furnishings also changed. Ceilings were redesigned to create visual impact, dark oak wall panelling disappeared behind

colourful paper and silk wall hangings, windows were raised and doors lowered – in short, no expense was spared.

The culmination of years of energy, skill and craftsmanship expended to realize Lady Louisa's vision for Castletown House can be admired in the Print Room, the only original room of this kind left in Ireland, and in the Long Gallery. The latter was redecorated in the 1770s and became a haven for private entertainment within a sophisticated Italianate setting. It was replete with Raphaelite paintings, Pompeian arabesques, exquisite Murano glass chandeliers that are unique in Ireland and a collection of classical busts and statues, all gathered under the benevolent eyes of the two owners' portraits at either end of the room.

Castletown House served as the ancestral home to successive generations of Conollys until 1965. Following its rescue by the fledgling Irish Georgian Society, and subsequent management by the Castletown Foundation, it has been owned and managed by the OPW since 1994. The Castletown Foundation owns much of the collection and continues to fulfil an advisory role on the interiors at Castletown.

A massive conservation programme of works commenced in 2000 and continues to this day, resulting in a new roof, new mechanical and electrical services and the conserved Kitchen Wing, which now houses the café. Since 2011, a new conference and cultural centre has been open in the Stable Wing. Here monthly craft fairs and country markets take place, as well as an antiques fair in the spring, while the atmospheric Hunting Room on the first floor hosts

CASTLETOWN

Celbridge
Co. Kildare

General Enquiries
+353 (0) 1 628 8252
castletown@opw.ie
www.castletownhouse.ie

Venue Hire & Events
castletownevents@opw.ie

concerts, film screenings and talks.

Great care has also been taken by the OPW in the restoration of the landscaped parklands, which extend towards the River Liffey and include meadows, waterways and woodlands with man-made accents carefully inserted into nature for the walker to discover and enjoy. Among these are a classical temple, a Gothic Revival lodge, clusters of once-rare imported trees dotting wide open spaces, still ponds, cascades and watercourses, all of which enhance the pleasure of outdoor activities around an extensive network of new paths. It is no surprise that Castletown has been recommended by *The Irish Times* as one of the top five destinations in the Dublin area to take your children for a walk.

In 2016, the Pleasure Grounds were restored and are now open to visitors to the House and farmyard. The latter is yet another achievement we owe to Lady Louisa's indefatigable entrepreneurial spirit. It is open during the summer months for the Castletown Experience, an offer especially tailored to families that includes a visiting pet farm, as well as access to a secure small play area.

Today, visitors to Castletown can enjoy a fine collection of Irish decorative arts within a setting that is famed both for its architectural significance and for the beauty of its natural environment. What is more, Castletown offers exciting changing exhibitions each year, as well as a vibrant year-round programme of events for all ages and tastes, from concerts to opera, from theatre to film, from readings and talks to hands-on workshops.

LADY LOUISA'S
BUREAU

A VIEW OF THE
HOUSE FROM THE
RIVER LIFFEY

THE PRINT ROOM

SCULPTURE OF
KATHERINE
CONOLLY, WIFE OF
SPEAKER WILLIAM
CONOLLY, BY
THOMAS CARTER

133

KILKENNY CASTLE

A towering ancient fortress that captures the spirit of Victorian living

COUNTY KILKENNY

Text by:
Dolores Gaffney

Previous page
THE CASTLE AS SEEN FROM THE PARK

THE DRAWING ROOM

Few buildings in Ireland can boast a longer history of continuous occupation than Kilkenny Castle. Founded soon after the Norman conquest of Ireland, the Castle has been rebuilt, extended and adapted to suit changing circumstances and uses over a period of 800 years.

Today, Kilkenny Castle is open to visitors all year round and is largely a Victorian remodelling of the thirteenth-century defensive Castle. Each year, hundreds of thousands of visitors come to see this grand country house and walk through its fifty acres of rolling parkland with mature trees and an abundance of wildlife. Other features include a formal terraced rose garden, woodlands and a man-made lake, which were added in the nineteenth century. There is also a tearoom, playground and several orienteering trails for visitors to enjoy.

Over the eight centuries of its existence, many additions and alterations have been made to the fabric of the building. The original Anglo-Norman stone Castle was built by William Marshal, 4th Earl of Pembroke during the first decade of the thirteenth century. Kilkenny Castle later became the principal Irish residence of the powerful Butler family for almost 600 years. Butler ownership began when James, 3rd Earl of Ormond purchased the Castle in about 1391, and lasted until 1967 when Arthur, 6th Marquess and 24th Earl of Ormonde, presented it to the people of Kilkenny.

Through the centuries, Kilkenny Castle has been a backdrop to great events and great lives. The Castle's history is full of larger-than-life characters like Richard Fitzgilbert de Clare (better known as 'Strongbow') and William Marshal, the great castle builder and regent of England. During the fourteenth century, Dame Alice Kyteler was imprisoned here; she was convicted of witchcraft and sentenced to be burned at the Market Cross in the High Street. James, 1st Duke of Ormond, Oliver Cromwell, King James II and King William III, each of whom were major players in seventeenth-century European politics, all spent time at Kilkenny Castle. In 1904, King Edward VII and Queen Alexandra were entertained there during one of their visits to Ireland. In 2017, this ancient Castle hosted royalty once again when HRH Charles, Prince of Wales and HRH Camilla, Duchess of Cornwall came to call.

Two world wars in the twentieth century transformed the entire social order throughout Europe. Ireland changed dramatically, and elite families like the Butlers found their political and economic power eroded due to these upheavals. Remaining in Kilkenny Castle was no longer viable and in 1935, the family took the decision to leave. The Castle was abandoned until 1967, when Arthur Butler formally handed it over to the Castle Restoration and Development Committee, for the nominal sum of £50.

The Castle has been in the care of the OPW since 1969, by which time a lack of basic maintenance had resulted in structural decay and dilapidation. The first phase of restoration in the 1970s saw the Picture Gallery wing refurbished. In the 1990s, the second phase restored interiors of the central block to the style of a grand

KILKENNY CASTLE

The Parade
Kilkenny

General Enquiries
+353 (0) 56 770 4100
bookingskilkennycastle@opw.ie
www.kilkennycastle.ie

Venue Hire & Events
+353 (0) 56 770 4108

country house of the 1830s. The third phase of restoration, completed in 2000, developed the Parade Tower wing as a purpose-built function and conference area.

The Parade Tower is now the dedicated events area of Kilkenny Castle, where old meets new and state-of-the-art facilities have been cleverly integrated into the entire west wing and two medieval towers. The wide range of events catered for include banquets, conferences and cultural events, as well as Civil and Humanist wedding ceremonies.

Within the walls of the Castle, the exuberant spirit of the Victorian age is faithfully brought to life. The suite of three reception rooms, the Ante Room, Drawing Room, and Library, with their patterned carpets, yellow silk wall hangings and authentically reproduced gilded pelmets, all capture a sense of 1830s splendour. Throughout the Castle, the carefully considered colour schemes provide a fine backdrop for a diverse collection, which includes the internationally important seventeenth-century Decius Mus tapestries. Another highlight is the collection of Ormonde family portraits, several of which take pride of place in the great Picture Gallery, with its hammer-beam roof that features hand painted Pre-Raphaelite figures and naturalistic scenes. The Oriental fashion of the nineteenth century is represented by the Chinese Bedroom and by various exotic furnishings found throughout the building.

The OPW's open-access policy at Kilkenny Castle facilitates a free programme of events throughout the year, including garden talks, music in the Picture Gallery and gardens, special presentations and workshops during Heritage Week and an engaging Christmas programme of events that complement the beautiful seasonal décor in both the period rooms and at the Parade Tower. A diverse and eclectic range of events are also facilitated at Kilkenny Castle's adjoining park, including the National Day of Commemoration service, classic car displays, triathlons, orienteering, and a weekly park run.

The Castle's interiors today capture the nineteenth-century lifestyle of the Butlers of Ormonde, while the architectural elements of the building and its historic landscaped parkland reflect a more varied history that spans a remarkable 800 years.

THE DECIUS MUS
TAPESTRIES

THE PICTURE
GALLERY

KILKENNY ARTS
FESTIVAL

EMO
COURT

*A sublime architectural set-piece with a
delightfully eclectic collection*

COUNTY LAOIS

Text by:
*Myles
Campbell*

Located in a quiet corner of Co. Laois, Emo Court is an elegant country house set among the rich pastures of the Irish midlands. At first glance, the architectural discipline of the House, which is complemented by the formality of its gardens, suggests a strict Neoclassical vision that has remained fixed over time. Yet in much the same way that Emo's gardens gradually yield to fluid forms where woodland meets water, the House's restrained façade conceals an unexpectedly eclectic mix of architectural motifs, paintings and furniture. Together, they tell a fascinating story of a great Irish estate's changing fortunes and functions over the centuries.

Emo Court was commissioned in 1790 by John Dawson, 1st Earl of Portarlington, as a replacement for the old family residence known as Dawson's Court. Having been elevated to the peerage in 1785, Dawson had begun a series of improvements on his lands in Co. Laois in the winter of 1786. These included the planting of 31,000 oak trees and 9,500 fir trees. Just a few years later, the creation of Emo Court, which was referred to by one observer as a 'magnificent new house', represented the culmination of Dawson's steadily evolving ambitions.

The architectural sophistication of Emo Court owes perhaps as much to the matrimonial obligations of its patron as it does to its principal architect, James Gandon. In 1778, Dawson had married Lady Caroline Stuart, the cultivated daughter of the 3rd Earl of Bute. A regular visitor at Ireland's greatest houses, Lady Caroline was struck by the artistic discernment exhibited there by her social counterparts. She reserved special praise for the 'very good taste' with which Lady Louisa Conolly had recently transformed Castletown House, Co. Kildare. By comparison, Dawson's Court was felt to be old-fashioned, uncomfortable and in 'the greatest disorder', with a smoke-filled drawing room and a 'whirlwind' in the library. The employment of Gandon, whose Neoclassical masterpieces such as the Four Courts and the Custom House were transforming the Dublin streetscape, would soon extend urbane sophistication to the Laois countryside.

By July 1792, it was reported that Gandon's new House was 'almost completed' but, ultimately, his vision was only partially realized and remained so after the death of the 1st Earl in 1798. Under the 2nd and 3rd Earls, additions and alterations by the London architect Lewis Vulliamy in the 1830s and the Dublin architect William Caldbeck in the 1860s, brought the House to completion. Many of these, such as Caldbeck's domed Rotunda with its marble pilasters and parquetry floor, complement Gandon's crisp classicism, but delightfully idiosyncratic features also punctuate the interiors. In the Drawing Room, there are two screens of striking Connemara marble columns. In the Library, there is an extraordinary chimneypiece with riotous carvings of putti frolicking among grapevines, as well as a Rococo ceiling, in which rigid geometry gives way to sinuous plaster ornament.

Over the decades, these grand surroundings were the setting not only for exclusive gatherings but also for great public celebrations that brought the local community together. In

EMO COURT

Emo
Co. Laois

General Enquiries
+353 (0) 57 862 6573
emocourt@opw.ie
www.heritageireland.ie

August 1897, a school fête in celebration of Queen Victoria's Diamond Jubilee brought together 1,200 guests for tea and cake, while in January 1912, a ball was given for 300 tenants. Despite the image created by these magnanimous gestures, the family's fortunes were by now in decline. In 1920, the 6th Earl of Portarlington sold the House to the Irish Land Commission and its contents were dispersed.

In 1930, Emo Court came into the ownership of the Society of Jesus. Although many of the House's features were removed to make it suitable for use as a novitiate, several were carefully stored by the Jesuits. In 1969, Emo was sold once again, this time to Major Cholmeley Dering Cholmeley-Harrison, who initiated a remarkable programme of renewal. This included the re-laying of the intricate parquetry floor in the Rotunda, the reinstatement of marble chimneypieces that had long been languishing in storage and the creation of a new arboretum. In September 1995, the President of Ireland, Mary Robinson, formally accepted Emo Court from Major Cholmeley-Harrison on behalf of the Irish nation.

Today, Emo occupies a special place in the portfolio of properties cared for by the OPW. As well as bearing testament to changing fashions from the eighteenth to the twentieth centuries, the House is a social time capsule that transports visitors back to the more recent times of Major Cholmeley-Harrison. A fine painting of figures beneath Roman ruins, by Jean Lemaire, a pair of magnificent Louis XV commodes, and an Irish mahogany settee with a lattice-work back are just some of the highlights to be seen.

Under the management of the OPW, the revival of Emo has continued. In 2012, the OPW opened an exhibition on the life and work of the photographer Father Frank Browne. As a Jesuit priest, Father Browne had been based at Emo Court from the 1930s until 1957. In his lifetime, he produced a body of photographic work that has shaped his legacy, internationally, as one of the pre-eminent photojournalists of the twentieth century. Photographs taken on board the RMS Titanic during its fateful maiden voyage, are among the many now enjoyed by Emo's visitors.

The eighteenth-century parklands at Emo Court extend to over 250 acres. Some of the original landscape features are associated with Dawson's Court but since that time, the landscape has evolved to include a formal garden situated close to the House. This gives way to a parkland setting displaying strong Picturesque influences. The parkland today is laid out in a naturalistic landscape style with open spaces and mature trees, to create vistas and conceal boundaries. One of the most memorable features of the grounds is the mile-long Wellingtonia Avenue planted by the 3rd Earl in 1853, following the introduction of the Giant redwood into Ireland.

For many, Emo Court's grounds continue to serve as a much-loved local amenity, and are enjoyed by over 300,000 visitors annually. As such, they keep alive a spirit of openness that once characterized so many of Emo's great community celebrations. It is this spirit that, perhaps, remains the most important legacy of Emo's founding family.

145

HEYWOOD
GARDENS

An Edwardian classical garden in a
romantic Georgian arcadia

COUNTY LAOIS

Text by:
Hugh
Carrigan

Heywood Gardens, extending to fifty acres in south Co. Laois, are a model of early twentieth-century formal garden design situated within an eighteenth-century parkland setting.

In 1773, Michael Frederick Trench, described as 'a gentleman of large fortune, and great taste in the Fine Arts', built himself a house near the village of Ballinakill, Co. Laois. Around his new house, which he named Heywood, Trench created a fashionable romantic landscape, within which are many carefully positioned follies, including a Gothic-style obelisk, a sham castle and an orangery.

Trench went to great lengths to procure materials for his park, reputedly transporting the windows of the fifteenth-century friary at Aghaboe, twenty kilometres away, to Heywood. Trees were carefully planted to frame views and create vistas and a sequence of lakes was created. When Trench died in 1836, Heywood was considered a perfect reflection of the romantic tradition of gardening at that time.

By the early twentieth century, Heywood had passed into the possession of Lieutenant Colonel Sir William Hutchinson Poë and his wife Mary Adelaide. In about 1906, they engaged the services of the pre-eminent English architect Sir Edwin Lutyens to create new formal gardens adjacent to the house at Heywood. Lutyens designed only three other gardens in Ireland, at Lambay Island, Howth Castle and Islandbridge, making Heywood all the more significant on account of its rarity.

Lutyens's Gardens were created on several levels adjacent to Heywood House. They consist of four elements, linked by a 150-metre long terrace. The main feature is an oval garden, which is surrounded by a high stone wall. This enchanting enclosure has three terraced borders dropping down to a central pool, surrounded by small fountains in the form of turtles spouting water. The terraces are planted with herbaceous perennials and roses, while the surrounding walls have circular windows that frame views out into the eighteenth-century landscape. A charming garden pavilion is situated opposite the entrance.

Leaving the oval garden, the visitor enters a pleached lime walk and a pergola overlooking the lake and surrounding landscape. Among the other attractions is a yew garden, composed of three compartments known as garden 'rooms', planted with rudbeckia, iris, hellebore and old shrub roses.

The Gardens at Heywood are typical of Lutyens's work, with massive stone walls, formal lawns, alleys and room-like spaces. Although Lutyens was in charge of the landscape design at Heywood, the planting is believed to have been planned by his close collaborator, the famous garden designer Gertrude Jekyll.

Like so many other Irish estates, Heywood experienced mixed fortunes in the last century. Having been acquired by the Salesian religious order in 1941, the House was lost in an accidental fire, in 1950, and a new school building was erected on a site adjacent to where it once stood. In

1993, the Gardens were transferred to state ownership and are now the responsibility of the OPW, which continues the tradition of fine gardening at Heywood to this day.

Visitors to the Gardens can experience two distinct types of designed historic landscape. Dotted with intriguing and enigmatic follies, the romantic parkland at Heywood is one of the most picturesque landscapes of its time, while the twentieth-century work of Lutyens contrasts with – yet complements – this original vision. Together, they form an important part of Ireland's gardening heritage.

HEYWOOD GARDENS

Ballinakill
Co. Laois

General Enquiries
+353 (0) 57 873 3563
heywoodgardens@opw.ie
www.heritageireland.ie

OLDBRIDGE HOUSE & THE BATTLE OF THE BOYNE VISITOR CENTRE

*The gateway to an epic Irish battle that shaped
the future of Europe*

COUNTY MEATH

Text by:
Aisling
Heffernan

Previous page
THE ENTRANCE
FRONT OF THE
HOUSE

THE OCTAGONAL
GARDEN

CANNON ON
DISPLAY

Situated on the banks of the River Boyne, just five kilometres west of the town of Drogheda, lies Oldbridge House. The House is believed to have been designed by the architect George Darley and was built in the mid-eighteenth century for the Coddington family. Following a careful programme of restoration and development, the House, its stables and adjoining gardens opened to the public in 2008 as a new visitor centre exploring the history and heritage of the Battle of the Boyne.

This famous battle is one of the defining moments in Irish history. Since the Reformation of the 1530s, society had been divided along religious lines, with supporters of the Established Protestant church in Ireland gaining the advantage over the country's Roman Catholic majority. When King Charles II died in 1685, he was succeeded by his Catholic brother, who ascended the throne as King James II. James attempted to introduce freedom of religion, which threatened many of those whose families had made gains under the reformed church. When James's wife gave birth to a male heir in 1688, many feared a permanent return to a Catholic monarchy and government.

James's daughter Mary was married to the Dutch Protestant prince, William of Orange. In November 1688, at the invitation of seven English lords, William landed in England at the head of an army and marched on London. James fled to France before later landing in Ireland in March 1689, hoping to regroup and, ultimately, to win back his throne.

In June 1690, William landed at Carrickfergus, Co. Antrim and began to march his army of 36,000 predominantly Protestant men, comprising English, Scottish, Irish, Dutch, Danish and French troops, south to capture the city of Dublin. James and his army of 24,000 mostly Catholic Irish soldiers, supplemented by 6,500 French troops sent by King Louis XIV, had marched north to meet this advance and withdrew to a defensive position on the southern bank of the River Boyne. On the morning of 1 July 1690, the two armies clashed at Oldbridge.

William attempted to encircle James's army by sending troops west, towards Rosnaree, to cross the river there. James mistook this as the main assault and sent about 16,000 men upstream in response, which left the centre of his army weakened and exposed. Here the Williamites pushed across the river and James's army attempted to defend its position, but was eventually forced to retreat towards Dublin.

The casualties of such a large battle were surprisingly small, only around 1,500 men, and James's army survived relatively intact. However, James quickly departed Dublin and fled to France, leaving his army, abandoned and demoralized, to fight on until the ultimate victory of William's forces at the Siege of Limerick in 1691. Victorious, William's government reinforced the laws against Catholics, ensuring their systematic exclusion from power until 1829.

Situated on 500 acres that take in much of the original

battlefield, Oldbridge House today provides an interpretative centre for those who wish to learn more about the Battle or to explore the battlefield itself. The extensive gardens have been restored and feature an unusual sunken octagonal garden, a peach house, an orchard and herbaceous borders, while a tearoom has been created adjacent to the old stable block. Throughout the year, outdoor theatre, workshops and events such as cavalry displays and musket demonstrations help to recreate a sense of what it might have been like on that fateful day in July 1690, when Ireland's and Europe's history changed forever.

OLDBRIDGE HOUSE & THE BATTLE OF THE BOYNE VISITOR CENTRE

Oldbridge
Drogheda
Co. Meath

General Enquiries
+353 (0) 41 980 9950
battleoftheboyne@opw.ie
www.battleoftheboyne.ie

JOHN F. KENNEDY ARBORETUM

A permanent living memorial to one of Ireland's most famous sons

COUNTY WEXFORD

Text by:
Matthew
Jebb

The visit of John F. Kennedy, President of the United States of America, to Ireland in June 1963 was a moment of great national pride, as well as a personal journey that he described as the 'best four days of my life'. His interest in Ireland gave the country an optimism for its future and world standing. In his address to the Oireachtas, Kennedy asserted that no larger nation had done more than Ireland 'to spark the cause of independence in America, indeed, around the world'.

Following Kennedy's untimely death just five months later, a number of Irish-American societies expressed the wish to establish a living tribute to him in Ireland. The Irish government suggested that this take the form of a national arboretum and secured 192 acres surrounding Ballysop House, just six kilometres from the Kennedy ancestral home at Dunganstown, Co. Wexford.

A committee was established to develop the Arboretum, ensuring that it would complement the National Botanic Gardens by placing a greater emphasis on comprehensive woody collections. The tree collection was planned in two interwoven botanical circuits, one of broadleaves and the other of conifers, minimizing the visual impact of bare foliage in winter. The Arboretum was formally opened on 29 May 1968, Kennedy's birthday. Over the years, many members of the Kennedy family have planted trees there to mark visits and significant anniversaries.

The Arboretum includes some 4,500 species and cultivars of trees and shrubs. A sinuous road runs for over three kilometres amongst these, providing ever-changing vistas of the tree collections. Twenty-two countries, with which Ireland had diplomatic relations, each sent gifts of trees and shrubs representative of their country to the Arboretum.

Along the northern perimeter of the site are some 200 forest plots. Each covers an area of one acre and comprises a single species of forestry tree. These provide information on the performance of different plantation species in the Irish climate, and are monitored regularly to determine their productivity. Along the western margin of the Arboretum is a set of provenance trails of major forestry tree species, including Sitka spruce, grand fir, lodgepole pine and Monterey pine.

The buildings of the Visitor Centre are constructed from western red cedar and their horizontal design blends into the landscape. There is a reception hall with displays explaining the role of the Arboretum, a lecture hall and a small exhibition on John F. Kennedy. A memorial fountain fashioned from a single block of Wicklow granite bears Kennedy's famous words: 'Ask not what your country can do for you – ask what you can do for your country'.

Within the Park there are a number of trails through areas of native woodland where red squirrels still thrive. An international phenological garden is part of a scheme to study the effect of climate on plants. It is one of five such gardens in Ireland and is part of a network across Europe. Daily observations are made of the first date on which leaves unfold, flowers open or leaves begin to fall. The

miniature train, which runs during the summer, is a popular attraction, as are the playground and adjacent café, which is open from May to September. There are also orienteering courses that have been set up by Waterford Orienteering.

The summit of Slievecoiltia can be accessed by road and gives panoramic views over parts of six nearby counties, from the distant Galtymore Mountains, eighty kilometres to the west on the Tipperary–Limerick border, to Croaghanmoira Mountain, seventy-four kilometres to the north-east at the southern end of the Wicklow Mountains.

JOHN F. KENNEDY ARBORETUM

New Ross
Co. Wexford

General Enquiries
+353 (0) 51 388 171
jfkarboretum@opw.ie
www.heritageireland.ie

NATIONAL BOTANIC GARDENS, KILMACURRAGH

*A lush and exotic arboretum with a trove of
botanical treasures*

COUNTY WICKLOW

Text by:
*Matthew
Jebb*

Kilmacurragh House, in south Co. Wicklow, was home to seven generations of the Acton family. It was built in 1697 by Thomas Acton, whose father had come to Ireland as part of Oliver Cromwell's army, for which he was granted the lands surrounding the ruined abbey of St Mochorog. The five-bay Queen Anne house is thought to be the work of Sir William Robinson, who is better known today for his work at Marsh's Library, Dublin; the Royal Hospital, Kilmainham; Dublin Castle; and Charles Fort, Kinsale.

The garden was established from the earliest years, and today the remnants of the eighteenth-century, Dutch-style landscaped park survive, albeit considerably modified by later generations. In 1854, at the age of twenty-eight, Thomas Acton inherited the Kilmacurragh estate, the fifth generation of the family to do so. Along with his sister, Janet, Thomas had a passion for collecting plants. Whereas others undertook 'Grand Tours', travelling around the world to study art and architecture, the Actons departed from the norm and spent their time looking at trees across the Americas and Asia. Over the following fifty years, they established one of the finest arboreta in Ireland.

Their interest led to the early development of a friendship with David Moore, curator of the National Botanic Gardens at Glasnevin, Dublin. The Kilmacurragh Gardens became an unofficial annex to those at Glasnevin, growing plants that could not cope with the colder climate and the drier, alkaline soils of Dublin. It was through David Moore that Sir Joseph Hooker's collections from his Sikkim Himalaya expedition of 1848–49 reached Kilmacurragh.

There they formed the basis of what was to become Europe's most complete collection of rhododendrons from Sikkim, Bhutan and Nepal. Many of these rhododendrons have survived to the present day and have formed giant trees that give a dazzling floral display every spring. Amongst them, *Rhododendron falconeri*, *R. grande* and *R. griffithianum* still survive.

Following his father's death in 1879, Sir Frederick William Moore continued the family connection and took up the role of garden advisor at Kilmacurragh. The late nineteenth century was a golden era of botanical exploration and, through this friendship, the latest discoveries of the famous plant hunters reached Kilmacurragh, forming a remarkable collection of largely wild-origin plants. Together, Thomas Acton and Frederick William Moore created possibly the finest private plant collection in Ireland at the time.

Kilmacurragh's broad walk was planted in the 1870s with alternating rows of Irish yew, the crimson-flowered *Rhododendron* 'Altaclerense' and the lower-growing *Rhododendron* 'Cunningham's White'. Today this walk is one of the Garden's most magical features, especially in April when the fallen blossoms of the towering rhododendrons create a scarlet carpet on the walk below. The surrounding arboretum is notable for its collection of southern-hemisphere conifers. The local climate seems particularly conducive to the growth of a wide range of trees, and Kilmacurragh boasts many Irish champions – the largest of their kind on the island. They include, from Chile, the Patagonian cypress, Prince Albert's yew, Chilean

NATIONAL BOTANIC GARDENS, KILMACURRAGH

Kilbride
Co. Wicklow

General Enquiries
+353 (0) 404 48844
botanicgardens@opw.ie
www.botanicgardens.ie

totara and the willow-leaf podocarp; and from Tasmania, the King William pine, the smooth Tasmanian cedar and the summit cedar.

Two cultivars were also produced at Kilmacurragh while Thomas and Janet Acton gardened there. The best-known of these is the 'Kilmacurragh Variety' of Lawson cypress, an enormous specimen of which – possibly the original – grows along the old estate entrance avenue. The second, the cockscomb Japanese cedar, 'Kilmacurragh', forms a dome-shaped bush and the original tree grows in the Victorian double borders. Both Kilmacurragh cultivars originated before 1900.

Tragedy befell the Acton family following the death of Thomas in 1908. His thirty-two-year-old nephew, Captain Charles Annesley Acton, who had been born in Peshawar, India (now Pakistan), inherited Kilmacurragh. With the outbreak of the First World War in 1914, Charles and many of the gardeners at Kilmacurragh found themselves fighting in the fields of France on the Western Front. A year later, Charles was mortally wounded at Loos and Kilmacurragh passed to his only surviving brother, Major Reginald Thomas Ball-Acton. Just eight months later, Reginald too was killed in action, at Ypres, in May 1916.

Thus, in eight years Kilmacurragh had three consecutive owners, inflicting death duties amounting to 120 per cent of its value. This placed enormous financial pressures on the family and, after two centuries, the Actons were obliged to sell the estate. The House fell into ruin and

the arboretum became an overgrown wonderland of remarkable trees known to only a few. The state acquired Kilmacurragh in 1996 and, after fourteen years of careful restoration and planting, the arboretum was designated an extension of the National Botanic Gardens of Ireland in 2010. Notwithstanding this new prominence, the Gardens today retain a delightful air of ancient lushness and secrecy.

ONE OF THE MANY
VARIETIES OF
RHODODENDRON
IN BLOOM

TREES OLD
AND NEW

THE ARBORETUM
IN ITS WIDER
LANDSCAPE

163

THE ISLAND OF IRELAND PEACE PARK

A uniquely Irish memorial in the fields of western Belgium

BELGIUM

Text by:
Niamh
Guihen

The Island of Ireland Peace Park extends the reach of the OPW beyond the shores of Ireland. The Park is located on the outskirts of the town of Messines, near the French border in western Belgium. It commemorates all of the soldiers from the island of Ireland who died, who were wounded or who went 'missing in action' during the First World War.

The small memorial park is dominated by a round tower, thirty meters in height, which is intended to symbolize unity and to represent the four provinces of Ireland. Surrounding this tower are smaller structures, three of which list the dead, the missing and the wounded members of the Irish divisions who fought in the Great War. The round tower was chosen for its symbolic value. Such towers are a recognizable icon of Ireland from a time before political and religious divisions. It was felt that all social and political classes could readily identify with a symbol as universal as the round tower.

The idea for the Peace Park emerged in 1996 when Paddy Harte, a Donegal TD, visited the battlefields of the Somme and expressed a desire for the leaders of all parts of Ireland to commemorate the dead of the First World War, where they had fallen. Together with Glen Barr, Harte founded an organization called 'A Journey of Reconciliation Trust'. The goal of the Trust was to bring together Irish people by arranging visits to places in Flanders and to the battlefield of the Somme, where Catholics and Protestants, Nationalists and Unionists, had fought and died together.

Previous page
A VIEW OF THE PARK
THROUGH THE
TREES

MEMORIAL STONES
TO THE DEAD,
INJURED AND
MISSING

AN IRISH ROUND
TOWER IN THE
FIELDS OF BELGIUM

Messines was chosen as the most suitable site for a memorial, as during the Battle of Messines in June 1917, thousands of northern Irish Protestants from the 36th (Ulster) Division and southern Irish Catholics, from the 16th (Irish) Division, fought side by side in the same trenches. The story of Major William Redmond and Private John Meeke is often recounted as an example of this.

Fifty-six-year-old Major Redmond fought in the 16th (Irish) Division. As a Nationalist MP, and as the brother of John Redmond, leader of the Irish Parliamentary Party, he had dedicated himself to the cause of legislative independence for Ireland, known as Home Rule. Wounded in battle at Messines, he lay in 'no-man's land' between the frontlines, until he was spotted by Private John Meeke, a stretcher-bearer with the 36th (Ulster) Division. Meeke went to Redmond's aid and, while coming under heavy enemy machine-gun fire, managed to bandage his wounds. Private Meeke was awarded the Military Medal for his bravery. Unfortunately, Major Redmond later died from his injuries.

The land for the Park was bought in 1998 after talks with Messines Town Council, and on 26 June 1998, Paddy Harte and Glen Barr officially laid the first stone.

The Peace Park opened officially on 11 November 1998, eighty years after the end of the war. An inter-denominational service was accompanied by a choir convened specially for the occasion, of members from across the island of Ireland. At the Park, the Burgomaster of Messines greeted the heads of state – Her Excellency Mary McAleese, President of Ireland; Her Majesty Queen Elizabeth II of the United Kingdom; and Their Majesties King Albert II and Queen Paola of Belgium. President McAleese, in the presence of the other heads of state, unveiled a memorial plaque, dedicated to the memory of 'all those from the Island of Ireland who fought and died in the First World War'.

THE ISLAND OF IRELAND PEACE PARK

8957 Mesen
Belgium

Photo Credits

Arterra Picture Library / Alamy Stock Photo p. 167 top; Bernard van Giessen p. 154, p. 157, p. 161, p. 162 top right & bottom; Chris O'Neill p. 18, p. 21 top; Claude Thibault / Alamy Stock Photo p. 84; Con Brogan / OPW Photographic Unit p. 32 top right, p. 81, p. 82 top left & right, p. 94 top left & bottom; Country Life Picture Library p. 128, p. 131, p. 132 top right & bottom; Craig Stennett / Alamy Stock Photo p. 164; Davison & Associates p. 44, p. 47, p. 48 top left, p. 72, p. 75, p. 76, p. 82 bottom, p. 112, p. 115, p. 116, p. 132 top left, p. 133, p. 134, p. 137, p. 138 top; Dermot O'Donoghue p. 32 bottom; Design Pics Inc / Alamy Stock Photo p. 10, p. 28, p. 31, p. 32 top left, p. 90; Dolores McGovern p. 150; Donal Murphy Photography / Alamy Stock Photo p. 99 bottom; Doncha Ó Conchúir p. 127 top; dpa picture alliance / Alamy Stock Photo p. 88 top left; F1online digitale Bildogentur GmbH / Alamy Stock Photo p. 93; George Munday / Alamy Stock Photo p. 96, p. 146; Gerry Donoghue p. 88 bottom; Harry Weir Photography p. 34, p. 37, p. 38 top left; JK Photography, Tullow p. 149 top; Jonathan Hession cover image, p. 66, p. 69, p. 70 top left & right, p. 78, p. 140, p. 143, p. 144; Jurga Rakauskaite p. 53, p. 26 bottom; Kevin Foy / Alamy Stock Photo p. 100; Kim Haughton / Alamy Stock Photo p. 104 top left; Leon Farrell / Photocall Ireland p. 48 top right; Little Bug Media p. 21 bottom, p. 122 top right; Mary Griffin & Maureen Hanlon p.14, p.17; Maurice Savage / Alamy Picture Library p. 167 bottom; Maxwell Photography p. 40, p. 48 bottom, p. 99 top; Midpoint p. 127 bottom; Mike O'Toole p. 22, p. 25, p. 26, p. 50, p. 54 top left & bottom right; Myles Campbell p. 13; National Geographic Creative / Alamy Stock Photo p. 70 bottom; Pat Moore p. 138 bottom; Paul Cutler p. 9; Pauline Dowling p. 6; Photo Pool Maxpic / Alamy Stock Photo p. 38 top right; Richard Johnston p. 38 bottom, p. 39, p. 43, p. 56, p. 59, p. 60, p. 63, p. 64, p. 65, p. 87, p. 88 top right, p. 103, p. 104 top right & bottom, p. 105, p. 106; RM Floral / Alamy Stock Photo p. 149 bottom, p. 158; RM Ireland / Alamy Stock Photo p. 124; Rolf Richardson / Alamy Stock Photo p. 153 bottom; Ros Kavanagh p. 118, p. 122 top left & bottom; rumal / Alamy Stock Photo p. 109; Seamus O'Brien p. 162 top left; Shane Brennan, Moondance Productions p. 110 top left & bottom; Vincent Hyland p. 121.